50 QUIET MIRACLES

That Changed Lives

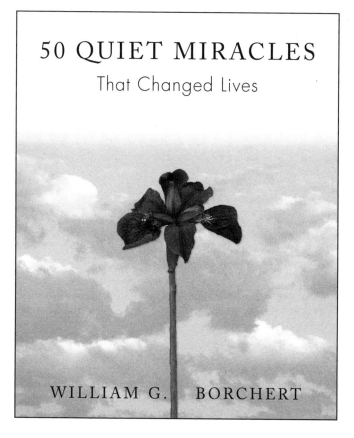

50 QUIET MIRACLES
That Changed Lives

WILLIAM G. BORCHERT

HAZELDEN®

Hazelden
Center City, Minnesota 55012
hazelden.org

Library of Congress Cataloging-in-Publication Data

Borchert, William G.
    50 quiet miracles that changed lives / William G. Borchert.
      p.   cm.
    ISBN 978-1-59285-750-0 (softcover)
    1. Christian life.   2. Life change events—Religious aspects—
  Christianity.   I. Title.   II. Title: Fifty quiet miracles that changed lives.
    BV4515.3.B67 2009
    204'.32—dc22

                                             2009022014

Editor's note
The stories in this book are based on actual experiences. The names and details have been changed to protect the privacy of the people involved.

   Alcoholics Anonymous, AA, and the Big Book are registered trademarks of Alcoholics Anonymous World Services, Inc.

13 12 11 10 09   1 2 3 4 5 6

Cover and interior design by David Spohn
Typesetting by BookMobile Design and Publishing Services

To my loving wife, Bernadette . . .
the miracle of my life.

Contents

Acknowledgments

I WISH TO thank those who have so generously contributed their wonderful "miracle" stories to this book so that others may share the reality of God's presence in our lives.

Introduction

MANY YEARS AGO as a young seminarian, I found myself kneeling amid the silence of a candlelit chapel as dawn approached asking myself, *If God were really here, why don't I feel His presence?*

Glancing around at the bowed heads of priests, nuns, and other seminarians, I became a bit envious, believing they had found some special connection to the Almighty that a sinner like myself could never find. Feeling spiritually inadequate, I left that religious life behind.

Still, I would often dream that perhaps someday I might witness a real miracle and my faith would come alive. I would then be as certain of God's spiritual presence as I was of the physical world surrounding me.

The problem for me was that miracles had to be awesome events, always accompanied by claps of thunder as someone rose from the dead or a crippled child walked or someone riddled with cancer or AIDS was suddenly pronounced cured by a bunch of doctors standing around totally baffled and confused.

I had no idea that God is constantly performing "quiet

miracles" every day in the lives of each and every one of us. If you're anything like I once was, then you're missing the soft whisper or quiet breeze while waiting for the thunderclap. You're brushing aside these experiences as mere coincidences, when in truth, this is God doing something for us that we could not do for ourselves.

Quiet miracles come in all sizes, shapes, and forms. They can be unexpected phone calls, chance meetings, a much-needed bank check, or a missed plane reservation that would have ended in disaster. They can be small enough to simply produce a warm glow or dramatic enough to create awe and wonder. And if we allow ourselves to look beyond the glow and focus on the wonder, we will recognize that, at that moment, we are in the presence of God.

That's what this book is all about: the stories of ordinary people experiencing out-of-the-ordinary encounters with something greater than themselves and coming to realize it's their Higher Power pointing them in a new direction, bringing someone special into their lives, solving a seemingly hopeless situation, or bringing calm into the middle of a raging storm.

Perhaps one of the most remarkable miracles involved a drunken stockbroker named Bill Wilson as he lay in a sanatorium fearing insanity or death. He reached out and begged a God he had little faith in to help him. Suddenly he felt the presence of God "as though the great clean wind of a mountain top blew through and through" and peace in his soul. His desire to drink left him. Bill went on to cofound the fellowship of Alcoholics Anonymous, which continues to save millions of lives all around the world from the disease of alcoholism.

It is hoped that these stories of God's miracles, big and small, may help to renew or reinforce your belief in a Power greater than yourself when you have been shaken by the worries and woes of the world around you. Perhaps they can provide tangible and meaningful evidence from the experiences of ordinary people that can help shore up the dikes of your faith so that you can begin to doubt less and hope more.

It has done that and more for all those who have shared their stories—anonymously but forthrightly—to make this book possible. I thank them for their great gifts.

I
God Calling

HE WAS EMBARRASSED, for some stupid reason, that his wife might see him on his knees praying, so Hank went into the bathroom and knelt down next to the commode. It wasn't an altogether unfamiliar position since less than three months ago his alcoholic drinking led him there quite frequently.

His Alcoholics Anonymous sponsor had been suggesting for some weeks now that the twenty-nine-year-old unemployed advertising executive start each day on his knees asking God to help keep him sober—and then thank God each night for another day without a drink. This morning was the first time he was following that suggestion. It felt awkward and a bit hypocritical since Hank and his Higher Power had only recently become reacquainted in the rooms of AA, and he hardly knew what to say. Also, he didn't want his wife, Sandi, to catch him at it, so it was a quick "Please, dear God, keep me sober today. Thanks." And then he hopped in the shower.

This wasn't the only big decision Hank had made this particular morning. He had been anxious and fearful about looking for another job since his reputation as a drunk was pretty well known in his industry, especially when someone would call one of his former employers. But with a wife and three children and a huge pile of debts, he had to find employment somewhere. So this was the day; with the help and urging of his sponsor, he had raised enough internal courage to finally go and start searching.

It turned out to be one of the most difficult days Hank had had since putting down the booze. Despite his highly recognized advertising skills and achievements, the problems his drinking had caused seemed to be the only thing people in the business remembered. He found a lot of doors closed in his face—most of them politely, but closed nevertheless.

Even his old drinking buddies who worked at various ad agencies around town were unwilling to lend a helping hand or put in a good word for him. He found them to be mostly fair weather friends now that he was no longer buying them scotch on the rocks. After a long day of rejection, Hank was ready to head for home and then to his local AA meeting.

There was a tasty-looking chocolate layer cake on the kitchen table when he entered the house. It was just what the doctor ordered—a nice big slice with a glob of vanilla ice cream to soothe the nerves and take away that familiar craving he was beginning to feel deep inside. Sandi walked in just as Hank had the cake knife in his hand and was ready to serve himself. She stopped him, saying rather huffily—or at least it seemed that way in the mood he was in—that she had baked the cake for her Al-Anon meeting that night and didn't want it cut.

Sometimes it doesn't take much for the disease of alcoholism to raise its ugly head, especially when you're only three months sober. Sandi's remark was the straw that seemed to break the camel's back on this terribly disappointing day.

Hank suddenly remembered that his brother-in-law had left four cans of beer in the kitchen cabinet after visiting over the weekend. He walked angrily to the cabinet, yanked open the door, grabbed a can of beer and popped it open. He yelled at his wife that he had had enough turndowns for one day and maybe he was better off drunk.

As he put the can of beer to his lips, the telephone rang. For some reason, he lowered the can and stared at his wife, whose eyes were filled with tears. The phone kept ringing. Finally, Hank picked it up. His sponsor was on the other end. He said he was on his way over to pick Hank up to go on a Twelve Step call with him to help another sick alcoholic.

The can of beer fell from Hank's hand. His eyes were also now filled with tears. He says he suddenly felt the presence of God all around him—the same God he had asked that morning to help keep him sober.

He knew it was God calling.

2
Saved to Save

IT WAS A VERY GLOOMY, rainy Monday afternoon as Martha, a forty-three-year-old housewife, sat in her bedroom finishing her fifth glass of wine and staring out at the hazy San Fernando Mountains that surrounded her lovely California home.

The large *Vogue* calendar on her dressing table read April 28, 1988. Next to it was a framed picture of her and her husband, from whom she was estranged after twenty-two years of marriage, mainly the result of frequent arguments about her drinking. So here she was alone and filled with self-pity while her three "selfish" children were off doing their own thing and not caring a whit about her welfare.

To get her mind off her problems, Martha went into her closet and dug out an old UCLA yearbook, the last one her picture was in before she dropped out of college to get married. As she paged through it, her depression grew worse. She saw the face of a beautiful eighteen-year-old girl, a girl full of promise, full of health, full of hope. There, next to her picture, was a scribbled note from one of her professors that read

"Martha is by far the most promising actress ever to come to UCLA from the state of Montana."

She closed the book and looked into the mirror. Staring back was a face lined with regret, with dark shadows under puffy red eyes, with lips that curled down in a grimace rather than upward in a smile. The pain inside was overwhelming—the pain of failure as a wife and mother, as a would-be actress, as a human being. *What more is there to live for?* she thought.

Martha went into the bathroom and opened the medicine cabinet. She grabbed the bottle of sleeping pills her doctor had prescribed for her just the other day. She went back and sat in front of the mirror again. Then she swallowed the whole bottle of pills and chased them down with another glass of wine.

Suddenly, as she heard a loud clap of thunder outside and the rain pouring down harder, she was overcome by fear. Suddenly she no longer wanted to die. *Dear God,* she thought, *what have I done? Please don't let me die.*

She ran to the phone on her night table and called her dearest friend, Betty, a lady who had been trying to get her to an Alcoholics Anonymous meeting for almost two years. The line was busy. She began to panic. She dialed her oldest daughter's apartment, but there was no answer. Her hands began to tremble and her face was wet with perspiration. She decided to call the police.

As she reached again for the phone, she heard the front door downstairs open and close. She rushed into the hallway. It was her youngest daughter, Annie, nineteen, who still lived with her. She had come home to get some clothes she had forgotten to bring to the cleaners. Martha screamed down at her, "I took some pills. Please, Annie, help me. I'm going to die!"

Annie half carried her mother to the car and sped five miles across town to the nearest hospital. By the time they arrived, Martha's right lung had collapsed and her liver and kidneys weren't functioning properly. It was touch and go for almost a week as her family reunited at her bedside to give her support.

The prayers of her family, many friends, and relatives, and the grace of a loving God, finally pulled her through. Martha and her husband did divorce the following year, but by then she was active in AA and much stronger physically, emotionally, and spiritually. She was able to handle the big changes in her life and move on.

While the divorce settlement left her comfortable, Betty, her AA sponsor, strongly suggested she find a job in order to keep busy and productive. Since Martha had some background in personnel work before having her children, she found a job with a major corporation working in their Employee Assistance Program, helping those with substance use problems. After a few months, the company decided to send her back to school to advance her knowledge about the various problems she would face in her new position.

She enrolled in addiction education at her old school, UCLA. Her first day back at the university, Martha found herself, strangely enough, in a suicide prevention workshop. While the instructor was speaking, she happened to glance down at the date on the worksheets she had been given. The date was April 28, 1991. It suddenly occurred to her that this was the exact date and almost the exact time of day that she had attempted suicide three years earlier.

Martha's eyes filled with tears. She knew it was no coincidence that Annie had come back that day to get the clothes for the cleaners. She knew it was the intervention of her Higher Power. She sat there overcome with gratitude to God for saving her life so that she could now help save others. As she turned and looked out the window, she noticed it wasn't gloomy or rainy like it was that day three years ago. Instead, the sky was blue and filled with sunshine—and she felt a glow inside. She knew she was in the presence of God.

3
Out of the Depths

IT WAS A TERRIBLE WAY OF LIFE for young black men like Stephen who, at the age of twenty-two, had been working deep in the bowels of a South African diamond mine for almost seven years. He would go to work already half drunk, feeling bitter and angry about the low wages and atrocious working conditions, with little hope for anything better in the future.

Stephen's father, who was an alcoholic for many years, had died recently. His son blamed it on a lifetime of slaving in the same dark, dank, smelly diamond pits that were now entombing him. But he had little choice. He was now his mother's only support, and he loved her dearly. She was kind and gentle and very religious. She was constantly begging her son to stop drinking, telling him that it would kill him just like it had his father.

To appease her, Stephen would accompany his mother to church on Sundays. Lately, however, it was getting to be a real struggle. He couldn't understand why anyone would want to worship a God who would allow people to live under such conditions and not even give them a chance for a better life.

Then one day the Maryknoll missionary priest who said Mass each Sunday asked Stephen to stay for a while so they could talk. Since the young man had taken a liking to the priest for some reason, he agreed. Little did Stephen know how much that conversation would eventually change his whole life.

The missionary confided to Stephen that he, too, once had a serious problem with alcohol, but that he had been sober now for almost ten years. The young man was stunned. The priest convinced Stephen to come to a local Alcoholics Anonymous meeting with him. He told Stephen that he had nothing to lose and possibly a lot to gain.

Stephen agreed and for a while managed to stay sober and develop a slightly more hopeful attitude. But the harsh, almost slavelike conditions in the diamond mine began to wear on him once again. The fragile faith in his Higher Power that he had begun to weave started to unravel, and his anger and self-pity returned one more time.

That was the negative frame of mind Stephen was in one day as his work shift ended deep down in the mine. Everyone rushed toward the lift to get up and out as quickly as possible. The lift was actually a large, rusting metal cage hanging from a cable that ran up and around a large wheel at the mine entrance, where an operator handled the controls.

There was always mayhem when the shift ended. There was a lot of angry pushing and shoving as everyone tried to scramble aboard. By the time Stephen reached the lift, it was already filled to capacity. He fought and cursed. Finally, as the cage began to rise, someone reached out with his leg and kicked Stephen off. He lay on the ground in a rage, watching the overcrowded lift struggle slowly up the narrow mine shaft.

The lift was already more than a hundred feet up when everyone down below heard a loud, terrible, eerie boom followed by shouts and screams. The cable had snapped and the cage was hurtling down toward the bottom of the deep shaft. The crash was horrible. All but two of some thirty miners were killed.

It was hours later before the lift was repaired and Stephen helped bring the broken bodies to the surface. It wasn't until he was off by himself, holding a hot cup of coffee in his trembling hands, that he finally realized what had happened. God had saved his life. He was shoved from the lift at the very last second for a reason. God had saved him for a reason—and something told him he had to find out why.

On his way home, he stopped at the small church and knelt in front of the wooden altar. He thanked his Higher Power for not only saving his life but also showing him how to live it—sober. Then he thought again about all those smashed bodies he helped carry from the mine—poor, hardworking men who didn't have much of a life when they were alive and now had no life at all. He knew something had to be done to change things. Maybe, he thought, that's why God preserved him—to try to help others, especially his fellow miners.

Stephen had a long talk with his friend, the missionary priest. Soon afterward, he joined the South African National

Committee and began fighting for better working conditions in South Africa's diamond mines. Later he would become a force in the bitter struggle against apartheid.

The miracle God had performed for Stephen deep in the bowels of a filthy diamond pit changed not only his life but also the lives of many others.

4
Friends to the End

THE CHURCH was quiet now. Everyone had slowly drifted out following the last service. Elizabeth, a woman in her late forties who was the church sacristan, began removing the altar linens and candles, preparing to close the church for the day.

She thought she was alone as she started to fold the long linen altar cloth, until she noticed a teenage girl kneeling in the rear pew. Each time Elizabeth glanced her way, the young girl seemed to be in more and more distress.

After putting the cloths and candles in the sacristy, Elizabeth checked one more time. The girl was still there, only this time she appeared to be weeping. Now deeply concerned, the woman slowly approached and asked if she could help in any way. The girl, Carrie, sixteen, began to cry even harder. Elizabeth sat down next to her and waited for her to calm down. Then they started to talk.

Carrie explained that her mother was a drug addict who had contracted HIV from a dirty needle a few years ago. It had now progressed to full-blown AIDS, and the treatments weren't working. Her mother was dying. They had little money and lived in a two-room walk-up, and Carrie didn't know what to do. So she came to church to beg for God's help.

Elizabeth understood the young girl's desperation, for she herself had had a serious drug addiction problem that cost her two marriages and a teenage son. She sat there for a long time holding Carrie in her arms, trying to comfort her and give her some hope. Soon they had become friends.

It was evening now and the church was quite dark. Elizabeth said she would buy her new young friend dinner and then bring some dinner home to her mother. For the first time, a tiny smile came to Carrie's face. Before leaving, she asked Elizabeth if she would talk to her mother about coming back to church and finding God again. The woman promised to do what she could.

After dinner, Carrie led Elizabeth to the run-down apartment building where she lived. When they entered the third-floor apartment and her mother walked slowly from the bedroom, Elizabeth stood there totally stunned. She couldn't believe her eyes, for she was staring at Jocelyn, who had been her closest friend growing up and throughout high school. They hadn't seen each other in years, not since Jocelyn ran off with a sailor she had only known a short time and got married. They moved to another state and Elizabeth never saw her again—until this very moment.

Elizabeth threw her arms around her once-closest friend. They both began to cry. Elizabeth could feel the presence of God in the room. They sat and talked for several hours. Then Jocelyn grew tried and weak. Elizabeth helped put her to bed and promised to come back in the morning.

Over the next six months, not a day went by that Elizabeth and Jocelyn didn't see each other or speak on the phone, often for hours on end. Elizabeth's love and deep faith bolstered her friend's spirit during a time when she needed it the most.

Through Elizabeth's counsel and great example, Jocelyn did come back to church. In the end, she was surrounded by her minister, her daughter, Elizabeth, and many new friends in the congregation who came to comfort her and help her leave this life with dignity to a far better one with her Creator.

To this day, Elizabeth and Carrie remain very close—as close as mother and daughter. And they both know it was God who reunited them all.

5
Lost and Found

MICHAEL, A FORTY-YEAR-OLD real estate developer, prided himself on being a "hard head" despite the fact that he was rapidly drinking his once-prosperous company into bankruptcy and coming close to losing his family and everything meaningful in his life. But no matter what anyone said, he wasn't going to join up with those "namby-pamby phonies" in that "stupid Holy-Roller outfit" called Alcoholic Anonymous.

Anger and resentment filled his gut, and self-will ran his life. He drank more and more to forget his problems, finding temporary relief in his stupors and blackouts. He was on a treadmill to disaster.

Only when his doctor showed him how swollen his liver was and told him his blood pressure was off the chart did he finally concede to attending a few AA meetings. But his denial was fierce, and if he really needed to stop drinking, he was convinced he could do it on his own. He didn't need any help.

One chilly and blustery Saturday morning, Michael woke with a start. His whole body ached. It was around 7:00 a.m., and he was crumpled up in the front seat of his car. Not only that, but his car was stuck in a ditch alongside a deserted country road. He had no idea where he was or how he got there. He had drunk himself into another alcoholic blackout where one continues to operate in a semiconscious state but later has no recollection of anything that happened during that period of time.

He had a terrible case of the shakes and sweats. His mouth was dry, his head throbbed, and his body felt like it was ready to explode. He straightened up in the seat, started the car, and tried to back out of the ditch. But the more he gunned the engine, the deeper the wheels dug into the soft earth. Finally he shut off the engine and angrily staggered out onto the road. He began cursing God as usual for getting him into another mess.

He stood there trying to figure out what to do next, which way to start walking, where he might find civilization. More than anything, he wanted another drink. He needed one desperately, for the shakes were just beginning. Then he saw a car approaching, the first one he had spotted since coming out of his stupor. He was greatly relieved—that is, until he glanced into the car and recognized the driver.

The man's name was Frank. He was someone who had spoken at one of the few AA meetings Michael had attended. Michael turned his head away as Frank approached. He pretended to be examining his car, hoping the man wouldn't recognize him.

When Frank offered to help, Michael stubbornly declined, saying he was waiting for a tow truck to arrive. The Good

Samaritan smiled. He knew it was a lie. He started toward his own car, then turned back and smiled again. "Are you sure there's no way I can help you?" he asked in a very kind and loving manner.

It was either Frank's words or demeanor, but something happened inside of Michael's head at that moment. He knew today it was his Higher Power making a decision for him that he could not make for himself. He looked directly at Frank, and his reply came from deep down inside: "I have a real problem with alcohol. I can't stop drinking, and I don't know what to do about it anymore. I'm dying inside. I know you're in AA because I've heard you speak at a meeting. Maybe you can tell me what to do."

"I'll show you instead," Frank said.

They left Michael's car in the ditch to be picked up later that day. They drove together back to Frank's house, where they had coffee and a long talk. That's when Michael learned that God had worked a miracle in his life that morning.

Frank had been on his way to play golf that day. He always took the main route to the golf course. But that morning he was so early he decided to take a more scenic road—a road he had never taken before in his life. It was a case of a sober AA member finding his way along a strange country road to pick up a lost alcoholic who was finally ready for God's help.

Michael has been sober ever since. He likes to drive that country road now and then because each time he does, he says he feels the presence of God.

6
In the Nick of Time

THEY WANTED TO MOVE to a better neighborhood so that their two young children could go to better schools and have a chance at a better life. But Sue and Mark's resources were limited.

So Mark worked an extra job for over a year while Sue cleaned houses and apartments every weekend. But even after they had scraped together every penny they had to put down on a lovely small home in the Chicago suburbs, they still had to borrow from Mark's parents and Sue's widowed mother, none of whom really had much to spare.

Finally all the papers were signed and their dream was about to come true. But a few days before closing on their mortgage, they received some bad news. The bank had refigured the taxes and title search, and they would have to come up with another $850. They didn't have it, and there was no one else they knew from whom they could borrow it.

They panicked. Not only would they not get the house, but they might well lose everything they had put down. They began to argue and blame each other for getting into this situation. Maybe they should have made the best of what they had. That night, as Sue knelt beside her bed, frightened and weeping softly, she closed her eyes and whispered, "Dear God, please help me to accept whatever your decision is."

The following afternoon, the day before the scheduled closing, Mark received a letter from his brother, Jack, whom he hadn't seen or spoken to in over a year because of his violent alcoholic temper and all the harm he had caused. Also, Jack had borrowed money from Mark in the past to finance his drinking and drugging and never paid it back.

Even though he had heard his brother was now in Alcoholics Anonymous, Mark simply threw the letter on the kitchen counter unopened. As he started to walk away, the phone rang. Sue answered. It was Jack asking if his letter arrived and could he speak with his brother. When Mark refused, Jack told Sue she needed to open the letter and then hung up.

"What does that bum want now?" Mark asked as his wife opened the envelope. When Sue pulled out the letter, something else fell out of the envelope. It was a check for $1,000. The letter from Jack explained the money was a partial payment on all the money his brother had loaned him in the past. It turned out to be more than enough money to cover their closing costs—and it came just in the nick of time.

Mark and Sue looked at each other, and their eyes filled with tears. They knew something strange and wonderful had just happened. Sue especially knew where this last-minute gift really came from. That night she got back down on her knees and said thank you to her most generous God.

7
Paradise Found

CANCÚN, MEXICO, is one of the most beautiful places in the world, and being with your husband at a gala sales convention should be sheer joy. But for Theresa, a forty-five-year-old wife, mother, and alcoholic, it almost turned out to be a nightmare.

Her husband, Sidney, an insurance executive, had been reluctant to bring Theresa with him this time because she had embarrassed him at gatherings such as this in the past—annual conferences that combined a modicum of business with a whole lot of pleasure. Only last year in Las Vegas, his wife had gotten so drunk and argumentative that she actually pushed one of the executives' wives into the swimming pool. Of course she later apologized and all was forgiven—but not forgotten.

Still, Sidney loved his wife, and now that she hadn't had a drink in almost ten months, his hopes were raised. She promised this time she would be on her best behavior, which meant no drinking. He wanted to believe her. Everything went well until that weekend.

It was Friday night, and Theresa found herself growing rather melancholy watching everyone singing, dancing, and drinking. She wasn't having any fun. Then she felt that old craving inside. So she snuck off for just one margarita. Then it was two. Then someone bought her a daiquiri, then another. Before long Theresa was on the dance floor doing a semi-striptease on the arm of an embarrassed waiter. Sidney was mortified. Everyone laughed as he grabbed his wife off the floor—everyone, that is, except Theresa, who kicked and screamed at her husband as he dragged her to their room and put her to bed.

The next afternoon, painfully hung over, the now-subdued Theresa strolled all alone down a pathway on the other side of the resort from where her husband's convention group was staying. She didn't want to see or be seen by anyone. But as she walked by a large meeting room, she suddenly heard uproarious laughter coming from inside. She thought perhaps it might be a show of some kind she could attend to pass the time.

As she approached, she saw a sign outside the door that read: "SVI Meeting." Curious, she stopped a passing room-service waiter and asked what "SVI" stood for.

He smiled and said, "It means Sober Vacations International, ma'am. All of those people are members of Alcoholics Anonymous. They don't drink anything, but they sure have a lot of fun."

Theresa thought about going in, but something made her hesitate. Perhaps it was the same thing that always made her hesitate anytime she thought about attending an AA meeting—her denial that she was an alcoholic. As she was about to walk away, a woman around her own age came strolling down the pathway toward the meeting room. Thinking Theresa was a member of the SVI group, she introduced herself and took Theresa by the arm. They entered the room filled with happy, smiling people.

Moments later, Theresa was sitting there feeling as comfortable as she had ever been. She listened intently to an AA speaker share his experience and feelings concerning his battle with the disease of alcoholism. She identified with everything he said. Theresa was so moved by the love they all showed her that she spent the last three days of her husband's convention attending morning, afternoon, and late evening AA meetings with SVI members there at the resort.

Sidney demanded to know where she was spending her time, so she took him to a meeting one afternoon. Before the meeting was over, his eyes were filled with tears. He had finally come to understand something about the disease his wife had been battling all these years.

When they returned home, Theresa not only joined an AA group in her community, but she and Sidney began signing up each year with Sober Vacations International. Somehow they both knew it was through SVI that God helped Theresa find sobriety in the paradise of Cancún, Mexico.

8
Two Bearded Angels

SOMETIMES WE CAN get so busy and so weighed down by the trivia of life that we lose perspective. We think we have to handle everything all by ourselves.

That was the path Rick was on until a near disaster brought him to his senses. The thirty-two-year-old television executive was working too hard, traveling too much, and looking too far ahead. He was starting to lose sight of what was really important in his life.

Rick had a beautiful and loving wife, five healthy and happy children, and a comfortable home that sat high up on a grassy knoll just outside of town. Yet he was taking it all for granted, seldom giving thanks to God anymore for all his wonderful blessings.

He and his wife, Barbara, just had a new son, and this particular Sunday morning, they planned to have him baptized at their nearby church. Perhaps anticipating this great event, the new baby awoke about 6:30 a.m., crying for his bottle. Barbara walked sleepily into the kitchen to get it from the refrigerator and warm it, only to find the room filled with smoke. Panicking, she ran quickly to wake her husband.

Rick leaped out of bed and headed for the kitchen in his pajamas. He started yanking open the kitchen cabinets, the doors to the pantry and laundry room, searching for the source of the smoke. Suddenly his wife heard a strange crackling noise coming from the attached garage. As she opened the entrance door, she screamed. The entire far sidewall of the garage was in flames.

Barbara ran into the bedrooms, dragged their children out of bed, wrapped them in blankets, and rushed them out into the backyard. Meanwhile Rick hurriedly drove their two cars out of the garage to prevent them from exploding. Then he grabbed the garden hose to put out the flames. It was a losing battle since there was no real force in the water line. The flames would soon burn through the kitchen wall and then spread throughout the house.

There was nothing left to do but call the fire department. As he started back to the house, he noticed an old pickup truck parked on the street below and two bearded men running up his long, steep driveway. Both of them were carrying large fire extinguishers. Without saying a word, they moved quickly into the garage and, within minutes, had the fire completely out.

While these two complete strangers were working on the fire, Rick moved to his wife and children to calm their fears and assure them that everything was under control. When he turned to walk back and thank his two bearded friends for their help, they were gone. He walked quickly past the garage to the top of the driveway to call down to them before they drove away. There was no sign of them or their truck.

Rick stood there scratching his head. He knew there was no way they could have possibly walked down the steep drive and left so quickly. It was only a matter of moments. And why didn't they stay around long enough for he and Barbara to thank them for saving their home and their family? They owed these men so much. How would they be able to repay them?

As he stood there staring down the driveway, his wife and children approached him. There was a look of wonder on Barbara's face as she quietly reminded her husband of the card they received from her mother congratulating their new son on his forthcoming baptism. The card showed two angels protecting a family from harm as they crossed a narrow bridge over a deep canyon.

Suddenly they both knew that God had just sent two of His angels to save them—two bearded angels.

That Sunday was a very special day in many ways. It was also a day when Rick stopped taking things for granted, realized he couldn't do everything himself, and started saying thank you again to a God more generous that he ever imagined.

9
Saved from 9/11

JUST HOW SHE was able to hold on to her rather important position in a large investment firm headquartered in New York City's World Trade Center was a mystery even to Adrienne herself. For by now, her alcoholic drinking combined with snorting cocaine was no secret to the few real friends she had left.

Almost every weekend, the attractive, auburn-haired twenty-seven-year-old would disappear into the bowels of the city's dizzying and often dangerous club scene. Then she'd crawl back out and come to in her apartment sometime on Sunday to sober up and face another boring week of necessary drudgery. At least that was the way she looked at her life at this point.

With that attitude now dominating her life, it was no wonder that everything near and dear to her was slowly slipping away. Most nights she'd stagger into her apartment after having "just a few" with the office crowd and not remember whether she had had dinner or not. In the morning, the mirror was her enemy.

Adrienne's manager at the investment firm was a gentle, caring middle-aged woman who had been her biggest fan since the day she started right out of college. But she was also someone who knew little about addiction. That's why she often appeared hurt and disappointed by Adrienne's behavior and kept trying to figure out what was wrong with this young lady who had so much potential.

Adrienne sensed her boss was nearing her wit's end because she was no longer buying the sometimes almost laughable excuses Adrienne would use after taking another sick day. As the inevitable drew closer, the young woman began to realize that not only was her career at stake but also her life was in jeopardy. She thought about asking for a leave of absence to enter an alcohol and drug rehab facility. She got serious and began researching rehabs the day after the boyfriend of one of her heavy-drinking girlfriends hung himself in a drunken stupor.

She managed to stay sober for the young man's funeral and also for a business trip she had to take to Denver the next day. The meetings there went so well that she joined in the celebration at dinner that night. Somehow she made it on to the plane that morning and drank her way home. She didn't remember where else she stopped upon her arrival, but she came out of a blackout around 5:00 a.m. sitting on the bottom step of her four-story walk-up apartment. As she tried to stand, her legs were like lead. There was a whirring noise in her head, and her heart was pounding in her chest. She was filled with fear, and though prayers were now like ashes on her tongue, she softly cried out, "Please God. If you help me get up these stairs to my apartment, I will do whatever you want me to do. Please help me get upstairs."

She finally made it up the four flights. She entered the apartment and leaned back against the door. She remembers saying aloud, "You will die if you ever drink again."

Adrienne staggered to her coffee table and looked down at the stack of brochures and admitting forms she had received from all the rehabs she had e-mailed for information. She picked one from the pile, dialed the phone number, and twelve hours later was checking into a rehab in western New Jersey. While a good friend drove her, she believes it was really the hand of God that got her there.

She felt peaceful at first, as though she had finally surrendered. But by the third day in detox, she was convinced she had made a huge mistake. Even though her manager at the investment firm said she understood and granted her a thirty-day leave of absence, Adrienne was certain she would lose her job or, at the very least, have the stigma of alcoholism on her record.

Then an incident occurred the following week that made her wonder if God really wanted her there, if He was still on her side. She was scheduled to meet again with one of the ministers who was associated with the rehab to continue discussing the spiritual program she had embarked on through the Twelve Step program of Alcoholics Anonymous. Today they were to discuss Step Three: "Made a decision to turn our will and our lives over to the care of God *as we understood Him.*"

Adrienne was looking forward to the meeting. She knew something had to change inside her if she had any chance of staying sober. The appointment was scheduled for 9:00 a.m. She sat and waited. By 9:30 a.m. all of her negative thinking began to kick in. By 9:45 she was convinced God was too busy for her and that maybe she should seriously consider leaving.

That's when she heard herself being paged on the intercom to come directly to her alcohol counselor's office. Still miffed, she headed down the hallway. She noticed people walking quickly past her with strange looks on their faces. She entered her counselor's office to find the recovery group she was assigned to all staring at the TV on the desk. Some were weeping. Others were pale and shaking.

Adrienne turned and looked at the TV. She saw both towers of the World Trade Center ablaze. Her counselor walked over and put her arm around her, whispering that two planes had just crashed into the towers, and it was now suspected to be a terrorist incident. As she spoke, suddenly one of the towers began tumbling to the ground. Everyone let out a blood-curdling scream.

Adrienne stumbled into a chair and began to weep hysterically. She was watching all of her co-workers and other friends she had in the World Trade Center die a horrible death right before her eyes. *This couldn't be happening,* she thought. *And if it is, why am I sitting here watching it when I should be there?*

She had some difficult days ahead of her, but she did manage to stay sober. It took some time to separate her anger against God for the tragedy of 9/11, which cost the lives of her friends and co-workers, from the gratitude she had for God saving her life.

In the end, Adrienne came to realize that God saved her for a purpose, which she eventually realized by helping others like herself find recovery from addiction to alcohol and other drugs.

10
Recognizing God's Miracles

WHEN THE CATHOLIC CHURCH ordains a priest, it is expected he will be a priest forever. So there is little or no preparation for employment in the outside world if a priest decides to leave his calling or is forced out because of circumstances that are unacceptable to his bishop and/or parishioners. That's the situation the former Father Jonathan found himself in as he walked the streets of San Francisco one cold January day wondering how he would get his next meal or a place to sleep.

Jonathan had been a respected priest in a large Colorado city for many years until the disease of alcoholism took control of his life. The local bishop began sending him to cloistered monasteries for months at a time, then to a series of alcohol rehabs. But nothing worked. The priest just couldn't seem to stay sober or avoid creating embarrassing situations in the parish.

As a last resort, he was sent to see a psychiatrist, who put him through a battery of psychological tests. The priest was told he had a lot of problems that psychiatry couldn't help.

When asked what he should do, he was told, "The picture is very grim. If you don't stop drinking, you will drift to a level in society where eventually you will have to be taken care of. You will then live out your life in a helpless state until you die—probably a violent death."

Jonathan, now in his early fifties, refused to accept the psychiatrist's diagnosis. He was determined that no such thing would happen to him. But he did nothing to change his way of life and continued drinking. After creating one too many unacceptable situations, the bishop had no choice but to dismiss him from the priesthood and send him out into a world with which he was ill prepared to cope.

Through a help-wanted ad he found at a local Salvation Army station, he wound up with a job in a smelly meat packing plant. Out of shame, he concealed his identity as an ex-priest from his fellow workers and others he came across. Shortly after being hired, the plant foreman pulled him aside to talk to him about his drinking. He expressed concern that Jonathan might cause an accident or injure himself on the job. The foreman suggested that Jonathan go to Alcoholics Anonymous, or he'd have to let him go. Little did the ex-priest know at the time that the foreman was a member of AA himself.

Jonathan had attended some AA meetings in the past only because he was forced to each time he left a rehab. While he felt it was beneath his priestly dignity at the time, now he was fearful of being fired, losing what little he had, and fulfilling the psychiatrist's grim prediction. So he went.

One of the foundations of AA's spiritual program is "rigorous honesty," so little by little, when asked about his background, Jonathan would let people in the meeting rooms know he had once been a Catholic priest. He expected them to be shocked, but they weren't. They simply smiled and encouraged him to keep coming. Some, however, wondered why such a well-educated man was working in a meat packing plant.

Soon the ex-priest had an AA sponsor and was practicing the program's Twelve Steps of recovery. One night after a meeting, he told his sponsor he'd like to leave the meat packing plant but didn't know what else he should try.

"If you keep turning your will and your life over to the care of your Higher Power," his sponsor replied, "I'm sure God will show you what He wants you to do when the time comes. In the meantime, He's giving you everything you need."

At this point, Jonathan was still struggling with his relationship with God because of all the guilt he still felt inside. He had once felt secure about his calling to be a priest. Now he wasn't sure what God wanted him to do. So he simply followed his sponsor's advice since doing so had kept him sober for some time now.

The former priest became a regular member of the Friday night meeting held at the city's Harbor Light Center. He enjoyed the camaraderie of an all-men gathering, where they could talk more openly about their character defects and shortcomings. After he was sober almost a year, the group elected him program chairman. His job was to get speakers from other AA groups in the area to share their recovery stories at Harbor Light Center.

One night, a middle-aged woman showed up at the group, not realizing it was a men-only meeting. As chairman, and still being rather new, Jonathan suggested to the others that they let her stay. It also happened to be a night when the outside speaker didn't show up and the group decided that he should share his recovery story. He reluctantly agreed. By now the revelation of his former priesthood was no problem. Even the lone woman at the meeting didn't seem surprised.

However, after the meeting she approached Jonathan and asked for his phone number. She said there was something important concerning the field of addiction that she wished to discuss with him privately.

The woman called him the following day, asking the ex-priest if he would be interested in working as a professional in the field of alcoholism and drug addiction. She was on the board of an organization that ran recovery homes for alcoholics and said her director would like to speak with him, if he was interested. Suddenly his sponsor's words came back to him—that somehow God would let him know when to leave the packing plant for something more meaningful on his path of sobriety.

He and the director met the following week. They had only spoken a few minutes when Jonathan knew that the job being offered to him as an assistant director would be a perfect fit. He would have a chance to share not only his recovery but also the renewed spiritual life he found in AA with others trying to climb out of the rubble into a new way of living sober. He accepted the job, and less than two years later, when the director retired, he accepted the position to run the organization.

One night as the former priest was walking home from a meeting that had focused on AA's Fourth Step of recovery—"Made a searching and fearless moral inventory of ourselves"—something struck him. It was something he realized his Higher Power had been trying to show him since that first day he walked into an AA meeting room.

He was initially turned off by the way people talked so casually about "miracles." They cheapened the word, in his estimation, by calling things miracles that, to him, were mere coincidences. Perhaps it was his religious training, because for Jonathan, a miracle had to be something grand—the sun stands still in the sky, the Red Sea is parted, or at the very least, someone is inexplicably cured of a deadly disease. Here AA members were talking about miracles as though they were acorns dropping from trees.

As he paused that evening and stared up at the star-filled sky, he realized they were right and he was wrong. He thought about the dozens of miracles that had already taken place in his life which he had pushed aside as simply coincidences.

He thought about the psychiatrist who predicted his demise, the plant foreman who just happened to be in AA and forced him to go, a caring sponsor who helped him understand how God speaks to us, the loss of false pride that once kept him from talking about his former priesthood, the woman who showed up at his group the night the speaker didn't come and he had to share his own recovery story, her happening to be on the board of a recovery organization that led to him now carrying God's and AA's message of hope to hundreds who were once like himself.

Today Jonathan continues to quote the Big Book of Alcoholics Anonymous that says in early recovery, men and women will look upon some things as coincidences, but that in time, they will come to recognize them as quiet miracles that God is working in their lives.

11
God's Bumper Stickers

As SOON AS her mother called, Eleanor jumped into her car and hurried from her home in Westchester County, New York, to a hospital on Long Island, where her father had just been taken by ambulance. An aneurysm in an artery near his heart had burst, and he required immediate surgery. Her mother was distraught and needed her daughter with her right away.

Eleanor was an only child and her parents were now up in years. She and her husband had often urged them to come and live with them. They, too, only had one daughter, who was now in college, and besides, their home was quite spacious. But her parents were too proud and independent, qualities she'd otherwise loved and admired in her mom and dad.

As the usually self-secure fifty-two-year-old woman drove across the Throgs Neck Bridge that afternoon heading for Nassau County on Long Island, she was filled with apprehension. The fact that her husband, Tom, was on an overseas business trip only added to her stress and tension. Still, strangely enough, she also had a modicum of quiet confidence deep inside because she was able to be there now when her mother needed her. That hadn't always been the case.

There were some years in the recent past when her heavy drinking and total self-centeredness made her a daughter her parents couldn't always depend upon and a daughter they weren't always happy to have around. That was particularly true of her father, which led to some long periods of ill feelings and lack of communication.

But Eleanor was a sober woman now. She had been for more than a year and was working a spiritual program in her life to change her former way of thinking and living. As a result, she and her mother had grown close again, and even her relationship with her father was softening. In fact, when she celebrated her first anniversary of sobriety in Alcoholics Anonymous two months ago, her father was there. He hugged her and told her how happy he was that she had become "the Eleanor I used to know and love."

Suddenly, as she turned off the bridge onto the main highway, she was flooded with warm memories of her father—how he would take her on the merry-go-round in the park, buy her Italian ices on a hot summer day, and tell her stories of his family who came over from "the old country." Now he might die. She began to cry.

Her father was still in the operating room when she arrived at the hospital. Her mother fell into her arms, weeping. She had already been told by the surgeon that the only man she ever loved, her husband for more than fifty-five years, might not make it. All Eleanor could do was to share with her mother what her spiritual program had taught her—to pray for the acceptance of God's will, whatever it was.

Her father made it through the surgery but was in very critical condition. She and her mother stayed with him in the intensive care unit until later that evening. Then they drove to her parents' home, had a bite to eat, talked for a while, then went to bed. Eleanor didn't leave her mother until she was fast asleep. Then Eleanor went upstairs to her old room in that small house and fell across the bed sobbing. She was sure her father was going to die, and she felt completely helpless.

The next morning her father was still holding on. The doctor said it was a good sign. Since the news seemed to calm her mother, Eleanor decided to drive back to her Westchester home, get some clothes, and return either later that day or the next morning.

As she drove along the tree-lined Hutchinson River Parkway, tears kept running down her cheeks at the thought of her father dying. There had been times when she was drinking heavily that she didn't think she loved him at all or he loved her. But now she was deeply aware of how much she had always loved this kind and generous man, who had worked so hard so that she could have so much. Her eyes blurred from the tears. She should have pulled over and stopped. Instead, she tried to get her mind off her sadness by thinking about other things.

She thought about her lovely home surrounded by woods and a wonderful quiet. It was a place she truly loved, especially her living room with her favorite blue velvet wingback chair near the window, where shafts of light would stream in through the old oak tree in the garden. She thought about sitting in that chair when she arrived home and hopefully finding some peace and comfort the way she used to. So often she would cuddle in that chair with a bottle of wine. It would seem to settle her nerves, uplift her spirits, allow her to dream wonderful dreams. Yes, there was a time she could do that. *Perhaps I could do it again,* she thought.

Suddenly she felt calmer. Just the image of herself sitting in that wingback chair sipping a soothing glass of wine stilled her mind and gave her some comfort. As the urge for that drink grew stronger, a car abruptly swerved into her lane. They almost collided. It immediately brought Eleanor out of her drinking reverie and sparked her anger. She stepped on the gas to get closer to the driver who had cut her off.

As she neared the car, she was stunned when she noticed two bumper stickers on the rear. They read "This too shall pass" and "One day at a time." These were two AA slogans that had helped her stay sober for over a year. She was so overwhelmed by the sight of them that she had to slow her car and pull off onto the side of the highway. She stopped to catch her breath for she knew this was her Higher Power stepping in to save her life.

Once again she burst into tears, only this time the tears weren't for her father. They were for the enormous gratitude welling up inside her for God's intercession that put her thinking and feelings back on the right path. She knew right then and there that if she were to drink again, she'd be walking away from her mom and dad once more when they needed her and would lose everything else she cared about in her life.

After a few moments, she pulled herself together and drove the rest of the way home, feeling that the presence of God was with her all the way. When she arrived at the house, she never even looked into the living room or at that blue velvet wingback chair. She went straight to her bedroom, packed some clothes, then drove right back to the hospital to be with her mother.

Eleanor was at her father's bedside holding his hand when he passed away later that night. She would miss him, but she knew he was now in God's hands and she accepted God's will. She also knew that because of "God's bumper stickers," she would be here to comfort and care for her mother and continue to be a sober and loving woman for her own family.

12
God Uses Regular People

THIS WAS ALL Walt needed to end a particularly difficult day—to be stuck in traffic on a busy highway in Fort Collins, Colorado, just as the first flakes of an early December snowstorm began to fall.

A physician at one of the city's large hospice facilities, he had hoped to leave work early to beat the storm, but a very sick patient needed his help. Walt's deep compassion for the dying would never let him leave anyone in distress.

Suddenly, as the traffic inched ahead, his car began to choke and sputter. Then the engine died. He couldn't believe it. The car was less than a year old. He kept turning the key in the ignition, and it finally restarted. But it continued to choke and sputter. He was able to pull off into a nearby service station before the car died completely. Trying to look on the bright side, the physician was thankful to have a warm and dry place to stay while a mechanic checked his car.

He was told there would be at least a fifteen-minute wait before someone would be available to help him. There was a convenience store attached to the service station. As Walt approached to call his wife about his predicament, he noticed a young woman exit, walk toward an old station wagon crammed with three children and a bunch of suitcases, then suddenly fall to the ground. Fearing she may have slipped on some ice or tripped over a gas hose, the physician rushed over to see if she was injured.

When he got there, the woman was sitting on the ground sobbing. She told him she wasn't hurt but still kept sobbing. She looked rather haggard, with dark circles under her sad and frightened eyes. He guessed she couldn't be more than thirty years old, if that.

As the physician helped her to her feet, a nickel fell from her hand. She quickly bent over to retrieve it, putting it with the rest of the coins clutched in her trembling fingers. That's when he noticed the gas pump next to her car read $7.85. He quickly diagnosed the situation. This young lady and her children were apparently in a desperate financial situation.

She looked up at him, saying, "I don't want my children to see me crying. I keep telling them everything's going to be okay."

Walt took her hand and led her behind the gas pump so they could talk more privately. When he asked again if she was all right after falling onto the hard pavement, her response stunned him.

"I didn't fall," she replied. "I got down on my knees to beg God for help. I didn't know what else to do."

The physician smiled warmly and said, "God heard you. That's why he sent me." Then he took out his credit card and stuck it into the card reader on the gas pump to fill up her car. While it was fueling, he led her to the food counter in the convenience store. He bought two big bags of food, some gift certificates she could use on the road, and two big cups of hot coffee, one for each of them.

While her children ate hungrily, they stood next to her car talking. The young woman said her name was Maggie and that she lived in Kansas City. Her boyfriend left two months ago, and she wasn't able to make ends meet. After falling two months behind on the rent, she called her parents out of desperation. They lived in California. She hadn't spoken to them in almost five years because they disapproved of her unmarried lifestyle. She was surprised and deeply grateful when her parents asked her to come home and live with them until she got back on her feet.

So she packed everything she owned, crammed it all into her old station wagon, and told her children they'd be celebrating Christmas in California. She didn't want to take any money from her parents for the trip, so she sold a few things, hoping the money would be enough to get her there. But it wasn't. Now she didn't even have enough left for gas, let alone food.

The physician reached into his pocket and gave her the $120 he had in cash. He also gave her his gloves. Then he hugged the young woman and said a quick prayer with her that God would watch over them the rest of the way.

"Are you an angel or something?" Maggie asked, her eyes filled with tears.

"No, sweetheart," Walt replied. "At this time of the year, angels are really busy, so sometimes God uses regular people."

As he watched the young woman and her children drive

away, the caring physician thought to himself how incredible it was to be part of someone else's miracle, how God had sent him in answer to her prayers. But God didn't forget about Walt either.

The physician's car was still parked where he had left it. For some reason he walked over, got in, and turned the key in the ignition. It started right up. He revved the gas. There was no choking or sputtering. So he decided to head for home, thinking to himself, *I'll put the car in the shop tomorrow for a checkup, but I suspect the mechanic won't find anything wrong.*

And sure enough, the next day, the mechanic didn't find anything wrong.

13
Final Payment

IT WAS RAINING heavily outside as Gary stood next to the hospital bed watching his closest friend struggle for each breath. Tim was in a coma, dying of brain cancer. Gary had been visiting every day since Tim was brought back to the hospital because he owed his wonderful friend a great personal debt. But how was he to repay him now?

Gary and Tim had been friends since they were fourteen, when they had met in a Maryknoll missionary seminary school more than fifty years before. Each thought they had a calling to the Catholic priesthood. They studied together, played sports together, did manual chores together, and both even wrote and edited the school's monthly magazine. They built a bond of friendship that was to endure throughout all the challenging and sometimes difficult years that followed.

Gary left the seminary after four years of study while Tim continued on for another two. They reunited at a fraternity gathering of former Maryknoll seminarians and drew close once again.

Since both loved to write, they found jobs in similar professions. Gary wrote for newspapers, magazines, and radio while Tim joined an international charitable organization, writing all its brochures and newsletters and handling its public communications. When they married, their wives and families became close as well and visited each other often.

As the years passed and his financial needs grew, Gary left the media and became head of public relations for a major corporation. He enticed Tim to join him as his right-hand man. Then later, when Gary founded his own public relations organization, Tim came along to help him manage the firm.

But financial success wasn't something Gary was able to handle very well. He thought entertaining clients was the most important part of his job. Soon his drinking became a major problem. If it weren't for Tim's strong support and patient understanding—both personally and in business—the public relations firm might well have gone under, and Gary's family would have been devastated.

When Gary finally sobered up in Alcoholics Anonymous, he knew deep inside that he owed his friend a great debt—a debt that could not be repaid simply with money or material things. He owed Tim much more than that for all his caring love and understanding during the most difficult time of his life. It had to be repaid in some very special way.

As part of his AA recovery program, Gary had turned his will and his life over to the care of God and was trying to lead a spiritual life. He had also begun to practice his Catholic faith again after drifting away from it through his addiction to alcohol. But the same was not true of Tim.

For some reason, his best friend had also left the church—in fact, he had walked away from God completely. All Tim would say was that he had become totally disillusioned with the world around him. He felt if God were truly loving and caring about His creation, He wouldn't be letting such terrible things happen to people and the planet. Then Tim was diagnosed with lung cancer, and his disillusionment turned into anger and his anger into agnosticism. He wasn't sure anymore if God really existed.

Things only got worse when the lung cancer metastasized to his brain. The treatments no longer worked. Now Tim lay in his hospital bed heavily sedated and, according to his cancer specialist, only a few short days from death. And Gary sat beside him knowing he still owed this dear friend a great debt.

As he prayed to God to forgive his friend's spiritual lapse, he heard a voice inside telling him what he must do. Even though Tim had stopped practicing his faith, he was still a Catholic. And in the Catholic church, there is a sacrament called extreme unction—also known as anointing of the sick or last rites—where a priest can anoint someone who is dying and give the person absolution for all his or her sins.

Yes, Gary thought. *That's how I can repay my debt to my friend. But where can I find a priest?* He decided to go down to the hospital lobby and ask someone at the information desk for the address of the nearest church. Then he'd rush over and convince a priest to come with him to his friend's bedside and perform the sacrament.

So he rushed out of the room and ran down the hallway to

the elevator. He pushed the button. When the elevator doors opened, Gary couldn't believe his eyes. There in the crowded elevator stood a Catholic priest. Holding open the doors, he reached in, grabbed the priest by the arm and shouted, "Hurry, Father! It's an emergency."

Stunned at first, the priest stepped out of the elevator and glanced around, trying to see where the emergency was. He was the chaplain at the hospital and was making rounds to visit the sick. Gary began explaining the situation as he led the chaplain back down the hall to Tim's room. But just before they entered, the priest stopped and told Gary that he could only give his friend the last rites if his immediate family requested it. The problem was, Tim's wife had also turned against the church, and she would never approve of what Gary was trying to do.

Gary's eyes filled with tears. He began to plead his case, explaining their long friendship, their days together in the seminary, how much his friend had done for him, and how the disease of cancer had now warped his friend's thinking. He said he knew deep down that Tim still loved his Creator and that God certainly still loved him.

The priest agreed, saying he was sure that God wouldn't mind him bending the rules just a bit. He entered the room, took out the small packet of sacred oils from his coat pocket, opened his prayer book, and leaned close to Tim's ear. He began whispering the prayers of repentance and absolution. Gary stepped back as the tears continued to roll down his face.

He turned toward the window and noticed the rain had now stopped. He looked toward the sky and softly thanked his Higher Power for showing him how to make the final payment on his great debt to his closest and dearest friend.

14
A Movie of His Life

BEING A RECOVERING alcoholic in the festive city of New Orleans was difficult enough. But hosting cocktail parties and tours of the wild and rollicking French Quarter for a bunch of heavy-drinking, hell-bent insurance agents at a company sales convention was putting a real strain on Chris's newfound sobriety. His wife, Jenny, could see it in his short temper and his satirical remarks.

At the same time, however, being head of public relations and advertising for one of the largest insurance companies in the South was the best job Chris had had since crawling out of a basement apartment and into the rooms of Alcoholics Anonymous ten months ago. And he only got the well-paying position because a highly respected business executive still believed in him and recommended him to the president of the insurance company.

By the age of thirty-one, Chris had already drunk his way off the staff of a big city newspaper and out of a great job writing syndicated radio shows. He had separated from his beautiful young wife and two children and moved in with an old drinking buddy in a run-down basement apartment. He was barely hanging on to a job with a small Broadway publicity agency. That's when Jenny called.

His wife had never stopped loving him or hoping someday he'd become just as disgusted with the life he was living as she was. He had almost reached that point when she called and convinced him to enter an alcohol and drug rehab. It was at the rehab where he learned he was powerless over the first drink and accepted the fact that drinking had made his life unmanageable. When he left the rehab, he joined AA, got a sponsor, and began working the program's Twelve Steps of recovery.

When he was first offered the public relations position at the company's headquarters in Atlanta, Georgia, it wasn't an easy decision to move away from family and friends to a new city and new surroundings, especially for Jenny and the children. But Jenny realized it meant a new start for her husband, and she was hopeful for the future after all the problems of the past.

Chris immediately joined an AA group in Atlanta and began making a name for himself at his new company. The president was pleased with his accomplishments and how he seemed to fit in with the executive staff. While the young public relations man knew that part of his job would be to plan, organize, and host two yearly sales conventions, he gave little thought at first as to what that responsibility really entailed: days filled with lots of drunken revelry.

So now here he was hosting the first such sales convention in New Orleans. Certainly there were some rather calm activities like city tours and shopping for those insurance agents who brought their spouses, but those who were single or had left their partners at home were looking to party. Chris had an assistant PR staffer to help him with the wining and dining, but most of it fell on his shoulders. For the first two nights, Jenny found herself alone in their hotel room, worrying.

By the third day, Chris had had it. So had his wife. She told him in no uncertain terms that he had to take some time out to attend an AA meeting. He reacted angrily, accusing her of sticking her nose in where it didn't belong. He stormed out of their room only to come back a short time later to apologize. It was early afternoon, so they decided to take a walk to calm down.

As they strolled down a tree-lined street near the hotel, Chris told Jenny that he had been praying like crazy to God to help him stay sober. He kissed his wife and thanked her again for all her support. Jenny kissed him back and said she was sure God would find a way to help him.

As they turned the corner, they spotted a movie theater across the street. For some reason Chris suggested they go see whatever movie was playing, just to get their minds off things. His wife agreed that it might help them relax.

Neither of them had heard anything about the movie that was playing there that day. It was *Days of Wine and Roses* starring Jack Lemmon and Lee Remick. It was about a public relations man who became an alcoholic and ruined his career and his family as a result. In the end he found AA and his way back into a sober life.

Chris and Jenny watched the movie with tears rolling down their faces. They both knew that this was no coincidence. They knew that God had brought them into this theater to show them what their lives had been like and what a wondrous gift He had given them—the gift of recovery.

Chris never had a problem staying sober from that day on. That's what often happens when people experience the presence of God in their lives.

15
Going Home

LEAH WAS DYING right in front of her mother's eyes, and Donna was powerless to do anything about it.

Until this morning, their "dream trip" to Australia, which Leah had always wanted to make, had turned out far better than either of them could have imagined. Now it was about to conclude on a tragic note.

"Please don't let it end like this, dear God," Donna prayed as her daughter lay weak and helpless on the couch in their hotel room. "Please just help us get back to South Carolina."

Leah was only fourteen when she contracted a rare and aggressive form of leukemia. Donna, a thirty-seven-year-old single mother, was a nurse. She went to every specialist she knew and others she was put in touch with hoping to find a cure for her daughter, whom she loved more than herself. Then her prayers were answered. A week before Leah's sixteenth birthday, the leading oncologist who was treating her said the cancer was in remission. What a great way to celebrate turning "sweet sixteen."

After graduating with honors from high school, Leah entered Duke University. At age eighteen, her goal was to become a veterinarian. She was crazy about animals. Donna was so proud of her daughter and grateful for her recovery and her promising future.

Then, just two months into Leah's freshman year, the cancer returned with a vengeance. A year of agonizing chemotherapy coupled with several experimental treatments didn't work. Finally the young woman bravely accepted the opinion of several highly experienced oncologists that the cancer had reached the incurable stage. Donna was devastated. As hard as she tried to accept God's will, she couldn't understand why He was taking her daughter.

There was one last thing Leah wanted to do while she was still strong enough to travel. She was a great admirer of Steve Irwin, Australia's world-famous "Crocodile Hunter." He was also a wildlife expert and conservationist. She had always dreamed of visiting the Australia Zoo that Steve owned and ran in Beerwah, Queensland.

While Donna didn't have much money left as a result of all the ancillary medical costs, she was determined to fulfill her daughter's final wish. So she cashed in her last CD, borrowed against her retirement plan, and set off for "Down Under."

Just to see the expression on her daughter's face when she met the Crocodile Hunter was worth every penny Donna scraped together to make the trip. When Steve learned about Leah's condition, he gave generously of his time and attention and introduced the young woman to every crocodile and other critter in his exciting habitat. But while they were enjoying every minute of it, Donna was watching her daughter grow weaker and weaker. The medication they had brought with them wasn't working. Donna could tell the end was drawing near.

When they flew to Brisbane to visit a museum devoted to animal art, which they planned to see as part of their trip, Leah took a turn for the worse. That's when Donna suggested they try to get an earlier flight home. Leah agreed. So Donna called the airline. She was stunned by its response. She was told there were no reservations available for the next three days and that because she and her daughter had special fare tickets, there would be an additional charge of $700 to change their time of departure.

Donna didn't have the money. Even her credit card was almost tapped out. In fact, she barely had enough cash left to eat for a few days and then pay for a cab to the airport. Seven hundred more dollars was out of the question. In desperation she approached the hotel manager. When she explained her situation, the sympathetic manager suggested she talk directly with one of the airline's executives—in person, not on the phone.

Donna said she had no money to travel any distance at this point. The hotel manager smiled and said, "It just so happens that your airline's corporate office is only two blocks away. Isn't that a fortunate coincidence?"

On hearing this, the distraught mother began to sense a calming feeling inside. She knew it was no coincidence that the airline's executive office was nearby. She felt this was God's way of answering her prayers and that everything would turn out all right. It did.

One of the airline's understanding managers wasted no time solving Donna's dilemma. The very next morning he had a limousine take her and Leah to the airport and flew them home in two large, comfortable first-class seats.

Ten days later Leah died in her own bed at her South Carolina home at the age of nineteen. While Donna still misses her daughter terribly, she says she no longer blames God for her passing. Instead she tells everyone that their experience together in Australia and especially the circumstances of their returning home brought her even closer to her loving God.

16
Success Is a Journey

THE AVENUE OF THE AMERICAS in midtown Manhattan was jammed with people pouring out of office buildings on their way to lunch. Maneuvering his way through the crowd, Larry felt his anger rising each time he was jostled by another passerby. The unemployed thirty-three-year-old writer was in a place he really didn't want to be.

Larry had taken the subway into the city from Brooklyn that morning to look for a job. He had been putting it off for almost two months now, ever since crawling back into the rooms of Alcoholics Anonymous one more time. His unemployment benefits had run out, the rent on his small studio apartment was overdue, and the few bucks he had left in his pocket might last until the end of the week—that is, if he confined his diet to soda pop and potato chips.

As the stern-faced young man whiffed the aroma of fresh-baked pizza coming from a nearby Italian restaurant, he wondered where he'd be if his AA sponsor hadn't been buying him dinner almost every night. He'd probably be scrounging through the garbage cans behind Burger King like his friend Big Ed, who had given up on the Twelve Step recovery program.

Last night Larry's sponsor told him in no uncertain terms to get his lazy behind off the couch and go out and find himself a job—any job. It wasn't that the former writer was lazy. Far from it. In fact, before the disease of alcoholism took control of his life, he was one of the most ambitious and hard-working journalists in the media business. By the age of twenty, he was already one of the top reporters for one of New York City's largest newspapers. By the time he was twenty-five, he was a byline writer covering the day's biggest stories. That's when his drinking and big ego began to create serious problems in his life.

After a major run-in with the paper's city editor, Larry quit and joined the staff of a weekly news magazine that had been courting him for a while, unaware of his heavy drinking. His bigger salary and generous expense account supported even greater quantities of booze, which he gulped down in some of the sleaziest bars in lower Manhattan.

Soon he was coming home very drunk or not coming home at all, which led to a serious rift in his marriage. So for his wife's sake, he tried going to AA. It didn't work. He tried again, for her. When she didn't seem to appreciate all he was giving up for her, he got drunk again. She asked him to leave. At the time, his alcoholic thinking told him it wasn't such a bad idea. He'd have more freedom to live his own life—which meant he could drink as much as he wanted.

Shortly after their separation, Larry's wife filed for divorce. That's when he really hit bottom. He lost his job at the magazine and drank himself into oblivion.

One day a retired cop who had befriended him at an AA meeting months before phoned his house to see how he was doing. His ex-wife had given the man his number. He called and simply asked Larry to give AA another try. Surveying the shambles that surrounded him, Larry agreed. He didn't realize at that moment that the God he had abandoned was about to work a miracle in his life.

The cop became his sponsor and soon convinced Larry that if he were willing to go to any lengths to stay sober and work the Twelve Steps of AA in his life, he could recover and become successful again. He heeded his sponsor's advice and did everything that was suggested. When it came to finding a job again, it wasn't that he was lazy. He was simply traumatized by the fear of rejection. He felt he had so damaged his reputation in the media by his chaotic drinking that no one would ever hire him again.

And now here he was in midtown Manhattan, the capital of the media industry. He had been walking the streets since 9:00 a.m. and still hadn't raised the courage to knock on the door of any newspaper, magazine, radio station, or other media outlet. The thought of a drink grew more appealing each time he passed another bar or liquor store or got jostled by another passerby.

As he crossed Forty-sixth Street, Larry happened to spot the midtown advertising office for the newspaper where he once worked. It was a small one-story building in the middle of the block right next to a Greek restaurant. As a reporter, he would stop there occasionally to call in a story or to check some back editions of the paper for information on a story he was covering.

Perhaps out of nostalgia, he started walking toward the building. All of a sudden, he saw a man carrying a press photographer's camera walk out, stop, and light a cigarette. Then the man looked in Larry's direction. They both recognized each other at the very same time.

The man's name was Johnny, and he was a veteran photographer with whom Larry had often worked when covering stories. In fact, there was a period of almost a year when he rode with Johnny in the newspaper's radio car chasing police calls all over the city. Every time the young reporter had to call in his story to the city desk, he would ask his older colleague to pull up in front of a saloon so he could use the phone. Johnny would often kid him, saying that drugstores and candy stores had phones too.

The photographer grabbed his former cohort's hand and shook it warmly, asking how he was doing. Normally Larry's tendency would be to lie—to tell him how great everything was and then get away as quickly as possible. But for some reason, he simply looked at Johnny and told him his life was a total mess. He said his drinking had destroyed his career, his marriage, and everything he held near and dear. Then he explained he was in AA now, trying to put the pieces back together.

"When I was writing for the paper, Johnny," he said, his voice choking up, "I thought one day I'd be a great success, maybe a columnist or even the managing editor. Now I'm nothing but an absolute failure."

An understanding and sympathetic smile filled the photographer's face as he replied, "I've been sober in AA more than twenty years now, Larry. Remember all those times you made me pull up in front of those bars so you could call in your stories? I wanted to talk to you then about your drinking, but I knew you weren't ready to listen. I'm glad you are now."

The young writer stood there, stunned. He knew all this was more than a mere coincidence. He could tell by the comforting feeling he was getting inside. And he was no longer thinking about a drink. Then he heard Johnny say something that was to help him stay sober for a long time to come.

"Please stay in AA, Larry," his photographer friend urged, "and always remember this. Success is a journey, not a final destination. Each day you are sober and trying to live the way your Higher Power wants you to live, you are a success."

Before Larry and Johnny parted that day, the photographer told him he had a very good friend who ran a group of rather large suburban newspapers. Then he took his young friend back into the newspaper office and called the suburban editor. That afternoon, Larry had a job.

On his way home to Brooklyn that evening, the young writer knew everything that had happened that day— thinking about Big Ed eating out of garbage cans, bumping into Johnny, learning he was also in AA, hearing his wisdom about success, and then winding up with a good job—they added up to one of God's miracles—a miracle that changed his entire life.

17
God's Choice Became Her Choice

I<small>T WAS THE</small> first Saturday of June, and the air was filled with the smell of lilacs and roses. Shari and her husband, Ted, were driving home from the graduation ceremony at the high school where she taught. Ted turned to his wife and remarked how touched he was seeing her students surround her with their love, admiration, and gratitude.

"I could tell how much they really appreciate your unselfish sacrifices to help them succeed in life," he smiled.

Shari felt a warm glow deep inside as she listened to his words, particularly since her husband hadn't been her most ardent supporter when she decided ten years into their marriage to become a teacher. In fact, he thought it was just like those other fantasies she had failed at before.

But as Shari snuggled close to Ted, she began to think about the challenging journey she started out on some seven years ago. That's when it struck her that it wasn't all a series of coincidences, as she had once thought. No, it was a series of remarkable events that, taken together, added up to the quiet miracle that made it all possible, for she now realized that teaching had always been God's choice for her—and now it was her choice too.

Shari had been unhappy with her job at a large technology company. The pay and benefits were good, but the work was tedious and lacked any personal satisfaction with one exception. She had befriended a young woman who worked in the cafeteria who had difficulty reading. She began to help her. Soon the lady was calling her "Teach" and even suggested she'd make a wonderful teacher. For some reason the idea began to intrigue Shari.

However, the thought of going back to school in her late thirties while still keeping her job to pay the tuition seemed out of the question. She began to pray about it, wondering if it might be God's will. That's when a series of what she first deemed "coincidences" began.

Shari was transferred to another department at the company, which turned out to be "Remarkable Event #1." There she met a man who was going to law school at night while working the same hours she did during the day. He also happened to have a wife and two children to boot. Shari began chatting with him about the logistics of his pursuit and the possibility of her following a similar path to become a teacher. The man encouraged her to do so if she felt strongly enough about such a goal.

Shari knew that such a decision would require a strong personal commitment and have a significant impact on her home life. So she sat down with her husband after dinner one night to discuss it. She could tell almost immediately that he was opposed to the idea. He first suggested rather sarcastically that she was simply looking for "summers and snow days off." When she talked about the nobility and personal satisfaction that comes from teaching, Ted challenged her. Since they couldn't have children themselves, he said, how did she know she even liked children? And as a teacher, she would be surrounded by them every single day.

The remark hit a nerve. Not only had she been angry at God when she learned she couldn't have a child, but she always changed the subject when her husband would bring up the subject of adoption. Yet, she was very close to her nieces and nephews, whom she loved to take shopping and to the movies. So, after several nights of debating, Ted reluctantly agreed she should give it a try, since she felt so strongly about it.

Shari's older sister, a former dean of admissions at a prestigious university, suggested she take a basic writing course first since that would be a required skill. The would-be teacher discovered she could write pretty well. The next step was to find a college she could afford.

It had been eighteen years since Shari had dropped out of college to get married. She had been studying acting. Her older sister helped her find a state university nearby where, if she took no more than eleven credits per semester, she could pay a relatively low state residence tuition. It would be affordable. Not only that, the school accepted seventy-three of the seventy-nine credits Shari had from her acting program because of a recently created double major: communications/ theater arts in elementary education. She would, therefore, only need about fifty credits to complete the program. This was "Remarkable Event #2."

Three years into the program, Shari was told that one of the courses required to graduate was only offered during the day, not in the evening. She was in a quandary. She needed the income from her job to pay for school, and now it seemed her path to pursue her goal was at an end. Once again she prayed, knowing that if her pursuit were really God's will for her, He would somehow work it all out.

That's when she received a call from the admissions office. For the first time in the history of that state university, the required course in question would be offered in the evening: "Remarkable Event #3."

Shari was now convinced that when everything looks bleak, all you have to do is pray and then keep putting one foot in front of the other. God will do the rest. This again proved to be true when it came to the requirement of student teaching.

For the elementary education portion of her degree, Shari would have to be a student teacher for one semester. And since children attend school during the daytime, that's when she would have to teach. The only thing she could do was apply for a leave of absence from her job and try to skimp by on her husband's salary. Then came the shocking news. Ted lost his own job as a result of a company cutback. How would they pay the mortgage, her tuition, and all the other bills?

It just so happened that the head of the education department at Shari's state university had developed a special program to improve inner-city education and was looking for "adult learners" to teach the course. He felt Shari fit the bill. So she could teach in the "high needs district," and the university would not only pay her tuition but also a stipend so she could receive her degree without incurring any further debt. This was not only "Remarkable Event # 4" but proof positive to her of how closely God works in our lives if we ask for His help.

It was around this very same time, as she began her student teaching and Ted was still struggling to find a new job, that Shari's father had a heart attack and passed away. While he wasn't a wealthy man and had four other children, the amount he left her in his will helped them catch up on their mortgage payments and other bills as well. The week the money ran out, Ted got another job—and Shari got her first full-time teaching position: "Remarkable Event #5."

As the very grateful and elated teacher likes to say, her story doesn't have a happy ending because it hasn't ended. And the quiet miracles keep on coming. "I guess you might say the real miracle that all these remarkable events made possible is the relationship I have with all my students," Shari explains. "My genuine love for them honestly came as a bit of a surprise but a most satisfying one. I care for them as if they were my own children. Also, I had taxed my poor husband to the limit. Yet, while his support for my goal was reluctant at first, it has grown enormously as he saw and admired my determination and God's role in it. I love my job and I'm happier than I have ever been. I will be eternally grateful that this was God's choice for me because He has given me a great gift I could not have gotten by any power of my own."

18
Then the Clouds Parted

THE LATE OCTOBER afternoon had turned cold and blustery. That's why Fred was looking forward to the fresh, hot coffee he was brewing for the start of the 5:00 p.m. Alcoholics Anonymous meeting in the basement of this North Carolina church. As he reached for a cup, he spotted a girl in her late twenties enter the room with a younger man. They glanced around, then stared at each other not knowing what to do.

Fred approached. He extended his hand, asking if this was the first time they had been to a meeting of AA. The young lady nodded, then explained in broken English that she had finally convinced her younger brother, Alex, to come because he had a bad drinking problem—one that had already gotten him into serious trouble.

When asked if they would like to have a cup of coffee and discuss Alex's situation, the young lady said she'd rather wait for him in the car. This way her brother might feel more comfortable talking about his problems with people she was told would understand. Then she said something to her brother in Spanish and left.

It was a half hour before the meeting was to start, so Fred got some coffee and cookies for himself and Alex and led him to a seat in the corner. There they could talk without being disturbed. Even though Fred had no skills in Spanish, he was able to understand the young man as he struggled with his English.

A native of Guatemala, Alex said he had been drinking heavily and taking drugs since he was fourteen. Recently, while celebrating his twenty-first birthday at a neighborhood bar, he got so intoxicated that even his drinking buddies tried to stop him from driving home. But he wouldn't listen. Trying to beat a traffic light, he smashed into the passenger side of another car, killing the driver instantly—a minister returning from preaching at an evening church service.

Alex suffered a severe concussion and several broken ribs. He was charged with vehicular homicide, and when he left the hospital, he went immediately to jail. His parents put their home up to cover his bail and hire an attorney. It was the lawyer who suggested he attend some AA meetings while awaiting trial. He thought it might help Alex's case.

Fred suggested that whether it helped his case or not, he should join the AA program to take care of his drinking problem and save his own life. Alex's eyes filled with tears as he asked this kind man next to him, who had more than twenty years of sobriety, to help him. That was the beginning of a miraculous journey for both of them.

After the AA meeting ended, Fred bought his new, young sponsee a copy of the Big Book in Spanish and told him to start reading it. Then Fred walked him to his sister's car and strongly suggested he attend an AA meeting every single day. He said if his sister couldn't drive him, he'd pick him up. From that night to the day of his trial, Alex never missed a meeting.

Fred worked closely with the young man, taking him through the program's Twelve Steps of recovery. They often prayed together, especially for the minister who was killed in that tragic automobile accident. Picking Alex up at his house for meetings, Fred got to know the young man's parents and his siblings. He could tell the parents were fearful and con-fused but elated that this older man was helping their son.

One night Alex asked if Fred would talk about his father's concerns. His father was making arrangements for Alex to fly back to Guatemala and avoid the upcoming trial. He didn't trust the American justice system. As his parents looked on, Fred told Alex that if he didn't face up to a situation of his own making—regardless of the possible dire consequences—he would never be able to stay sober and would probably wind up leading a useless life filled with fear and drunken-ness. Without any hesitation, the young man said he would stay and stand trial for his crime.

All of his attorney's pleas had been denied, and the trial was now approaching. By now Alex was trying to work the Ninth Step of the AA program: "Made direct amends to such people wherever possible, except when to do so would injure them or others." He asked his sponsor how he could possibly make amends to the minister he killed. Fred suggested he write a letter to the family.

The young man did. He expressed his deep remorse, explained how he was trying to live a better, sober life, and said that he was praying each day for the man he killed. Then one Sunday afternoon, the day before the trial was to begin, Fred drove his young sponsee to the cemetery where the minister was buried. On the way, they bought some flowers to place on his grave.

By the time they arrived, the weather had turned chilly and nasty for a late March afternoon. The sky was gray, the wind was blowing, and there were even a few snow flurries in the air. As they exited the car and started walking toward the grave site, something strange began to happen. The dark gray clouds overhead began to part. The wind lessened. And when they reached the minister's grave, a beautiful ray of sunlight engulfed them.

Fred and Alex stared at each other. Their eyes began to moisten. Then as they knelt to pray for the minister and his family and also for God's mercy on this remorseful young man, they both felt the presence of God. It felt as if He were touching them and telling them that everything was going to be all right, that He had a plan for Alex's future. Fred could see a peaceful look come over his sponsee's face.

When they returned to the car a short time later, the sky had darkened once again and the wind and snow flurries resumed.

Alex was convicted of vehicular homicide and given a five-to seven-year sentence in state prison. He promised Fred he would continue to practice his AA program behind bars and kept that promise. In fact, he carried the message of sobriety by helping other Spanish-speaking prisoners and translating for them at meetings. When he was transferred to another prison, he started a Spanish-speaking meeting there and translated the Twelve Steps on paper for all who came to the meeting.

The young man was transferred two more times over the next year and a half. He started Spanish-speaking meetings in each new prison and was instrumental in convincing fellow inmates to attend.

Alex was released on probation after serving only four years. Fred drove Alex's family to the prison to pick him up. That same night they were together at an AA meeting. Alex went to welding school, got a good job, got married, and had a family. Today he leads a sober life, always seeking to help others in order to make reparation for his past.

Fred still remembers that day at the cemetery when the clouds parted and the ray of sunlight shone through. It will always remind him of how God's quiet miracles work in our lives to help us change so that we can help others do the same.

19
Speaking in the Right Tongue

BRIGIT WAS EAGERLY looking forward to the upcoming weekend. After being sober for almost three years, this would be the very first Alcoholics Anonymous convention she'd be attending—the Pacific Northwest Conference in Portland, Oregon.

It was particularly exciting since her husband, Ben, who was sober almost six years in the AA fellowship, had been asked to chair the opening meeting on Saturday morning. He then surprised her by asking if she would read the Twelve Steps of recovery at the meeting, which immediately started those butterflies fluttering around inside.

A native of Oslo, Norway, the lovely blond-haired lady met and married her husband in that beautiful Scandinavian country more than ten years before. He was a handsome and successful American businessman who headed the Norwegian operations of a large multinational corporation. It was about five years after he returned to the United States with his wife that Ben finally admitted he had a serious drinking problem. That's when he joined AA and found sobriety.

Brigit continued to live in denial of her own alcoholic drinking until it almost ruined their marriage. She finally surrendered, and their sobriety restored not only their relationship but also the deep love they once had for each other.

When they arrived at the Portland convention, they were not only surrounded by members from their home AA group but warmly surprised at how many people they knew from other groups in their area. In addition, the large hotel was filled with hundreds of program members from up and down the West Coast. Brigit was awed by this moving spectacle of sobriety.

However, the large crowd multiplied the butterflies in her stomach and increased her concern about the assignment Ben had given her—to read the Twelve Steps in English in front of all these people.

While Brigit had lived in the States for almost six years, she still had a rather heavy Norwegian accent. It was not only apparent, but it could obfuscate her words at times when she was reading in English, which she would have to do at the convention.

Brigit had already mastered reading the Preamble of AA aloud in English since she was often asked to do it at her home group. But she had never read the Twelve Steps aloud. Her plan at the convention was to spend some time alone in her hotel room Friday night practicing in front of a mirror.

That plan was foiled, however, when Ben and their friends dragged her into a convention hospitality suite for some "AA sharing" and then out to dinner. Upon their return, they all attended the opening Friday night speaker meeting and then discovered a "night owl" meeting, which went until almost midnight. By the time they returned to their room, she was too tired to practice reading anything. She promised herself she would do it first thing in the morning.

Morning came and Ben hurried her off to meet their friends for breakfast. Since the opening Saturday morning meeting wasn't to start until 10:00 a.m., Brigit thought she could eat quickly, excuse herself, and sneak off to practice for at least a half hour. She had managed to stick a wallet-sized copy of the Steps in her purse. But more and more people she knew kept showing up at their table to say hello. It was well after 9:00 a.m. when she was finally able to slip away.

Brigit found a chair in a secluded corner of the lobby. When she pulled the wallet-sized card from her purse, she was in for another shocker. She had taken the wrong card. They were the Twelve Steps all right, but they were written in Norwegian. As she stared at the card deeply perplexed, one of her closest friends in the fellowship, Rita, spotted her as she was passing through the lobby.

When her Norwegian friend started to explain her predicament, Rita began to laugh. She had often teased Brigit about being too uptight when it came to the way she spoke. But this time her laugh wasn't appreciated until Rita said, "Look, most people are still half asleep after being at those late meetings last night. Why don't you just read the Steps in Norwegian and either nobody will pay any attention, or you'll wake everybody up."

"I can't do that," Brigit replied. "What would Ben say?"

"Knowing what a practical joker he is, he'd probably get a kick out of it," her friend answered. "You're sober now, sweetheart. You can do anything you want, even speak in your own tongue. There are no rules against it."

Ben opened the meeting right on time. After reading the AA Preamble, he proudly introduced his wife to read the Twelve Steps. Brigit approached the podium. She caught Rita's eyes and winked. She introduced herself as a recovering alcoholic, gave her sobriety date, then held up her wallet-sized card, and began to read—in Norwegian.

As she recited the first two Steps, there was complete silence in the large room filled with more than seven hundred people. During the reading of the Third Step, a few people began to snicker, including her husband, Ben. By the end of the Fourth Step, there was a roar of laughter. Brigit finished reading the Fifth Step in her native tongue, then stopped, smiled at the audience, and said, "I was just checking to see if everyone was awake. I will now read the Steps in the language of their origin." The crowd applauded.

Brigit was told later that as she read the Steps in English, despite her heavy Norwegian accent, people at the convention never paid more attention to or understood the Steps better than they did that day. But that's not the real story of why this Norwegian lady's Higher Power made her decide that morning to read in her native tongue.

On that particular weekend, out on the Pacific Ocean, a fishing boat was homebound for Alaska. The skipper and his wife were Norwegian immigrants. The wife had been drinking for days. Something had to be done. The skipper told his wife he was altering course for Portland, the nearest large city, because this time he was going to get some help for her whether she liked the idea or not.

They came ashore, and he phoned AA's Central Office. He was told no one was available because the local members were all attending the AA convention at a downtown hotel. So the skipper helped his wife get cleaned up as best she could, then took her to the hotel in a taxi. They walked into the large ballroom just as the 10:00 a.m. AA meeting was getting underway. The woman looked around at all the people. They looked so happy and so clean. Could they really be alcoholics? They sat and listened.

The chairman called someone to read the Twelve Steps. A lovely blond lady began to read. It couldn't be! Was it really possible? The lady was reading in a familiar language— Norwegian. The skipper's wife heard the first three Steps and started to cry.

After the meeting ended, Brigit was ushered out into the lobby where another friend, Margie, was sitting with the woman from Alaska who was shaking and still crying. They took her for a cup of coffee, and Brigit was able to tell her about AA in her own native tongue. The woman and her husband stayed for the rest of the convention and then sailed back to Alaska.

The skipper's wife wrote to Brigit about three months later. She was still sober and attending meetings in Alaska. They continued to correspond.

20
The Mailman Delivers a Miracle

IT HAD TAKEN Todd almost two months of phone calls and letters together with recommendations from some top sales people he knew to finally arrange an interview with one of the leading executive recruiting firms in the city of Chicago. Now, after it was all set, he found himself worrying that they might dig too deep into his background and decide he isn't the type of candidate they could recommend.

As he straightened his tie in the bathroom mirror, the thirty-seven-year-old former sales executive for several large corporations was beginning to have serious doubts about even going for the interview. Yes, he needed a job. He needed one desperately. But he wondered if he was ready to handle the pressure that comes with a management sales position when his sobriety was still so tenuous.

Todd was only five months sober. Even his Alcoholics Anonymous sponsor, Ken, was questioning his decision making, suggesting that he look for a less stressful situation with a smaller company. But Todd's ego still loomed large, and his lack of finances to pay his overdue bills loomed even larger.

He hadn't gotten much sleep the night before, tossing and turning, trying to figure out how to explain a few big holes in his resume—those periods of unemployment between jobs due to his alcoholic drinking. Suddenly he noticed his hand was shaking. He was tempted to jump back into bed and pull the covers over his head. Then he remembered what his sponsor told him to do when those awful fears and anxieties hit. So he walked back into his bedroom, got down on his knees, and asked God to help him get through the day sober.

It was a beautiful spring morning as he left his apartment and headed for the train station. He tried to stay in a positive frame of mind. Also, he wanted to be early for his 3:00 p.m. meeting in order to make a good impression. But halfway to the station, those same old fears and that self-doubt started to return. Then the "committee" in his head began to chime in.

"With all the wreckage you left behind from your alcoholism," the committee was shouting, "like cheating on your expense accounts, falsifying meetings with alleged customers, drunken brawls at sales conventions, phony sick leaves, and a busted marriage on top of it all, who in their right mind would want to hire you?

"Yes, you always performed well, beat your quotas, and built your customer base at the companies you worked for," the committee added sarcastically, "but your track record at drinking always outweighed your track record at selling. That's why when you sensed the ax coming, you always quit before you were fired."

Todd's heart was now racing. Next came the cold sweats. It had become all so familiar over these past few months, every time the fear of rejection hit him. Next came the thought of a drink and how it would relax him and tell him he could always start looking for work tomorrow. He stopped and leaned against a lamppost to catch his breath. He tried to follow Ken's instructions—to think the drink through and then take some positive action to get the thought out of his mind.

Then Todd realized that the church where he and his wife were married ten years ago was right around the corner. He'd go there, talk with the minister, get some spiritual consolation, and he'd be fine. He actually ran to the church, hurried up the steps of the attached residence, and rang the bell. When the housekeeper answered, she seemed taken aback by Todd's sweaty appearance. He asked to see the minister and was told he was having lunch and couldn't be disturbed—that Todd should come back later. Then she closed the door.

What the alcoholic brain of this desperate former sales executive actually heard the housekeeper say was "Please leave. God's too busy to help you right now, so go find some way to help yourself."

When the church door seemed to slam in his face, Todd stopped fighting. As far as he was concerned, the demons of booze had won again. And the $40 he had in his pocket would help him find some solace elsewhere. Only once as he walked back down the street toward the busy thoroughfare lined with bars did he think what his sponsor, Ken, might say if he called him right now. He quickly convinced himself that whatever it might be, he had already tried it and it didn't work.

Todd was reluctant to walk into any of his former haunts.

He had bragged to his drinking buddies that he had joined AA and had started a new way of living. So he passed them and walked further down the avenue seeking a bar he hadn't frequented before. That's when he spotted Duffy's Tavern on a side street.

It was almost noon. The place was on the seamy side and smelled of stale beer. Three older gents were chatting amiably as they enjoyed their frosty cold brews. Todd walked to the end of the long bar and found a stool in the corner. The white-haired bartender with an Irish brogue welcomed him warmly.

"A shot and a beer," Todd said, not so warmly. The bartender sensed he wasn't in the mood for idle chatter, so he simply got him his drinks.

Around 12:30 p.m., the elderly gents and a few newer arrivals asked the bartender to turn on the TV so they could watch the Chicago Cubs baseball game. It was opening day. They all ordered more drinks. Todd was still staring at his. He hadn't touched the shot or the beer. Instead, he had been eyeing the other patrons, two with red bulbous noses and three with splotchy red cheeks. It was like staring into a futuristic alcoholic mirror.

Around the end of the second inning of the Cubs game, the bartender approached Todd with some trepidation.

"You want me to freshen your beer?" he asked. "It's gone flat."

"No, I don't think so," the sales executive replied. "Actually, I shouldn't be drinking at all. You see, I'm an alcoholic."

"Hell, that's okay, son," the white-haired Irishman smiled.

"I'm one too. But I control myself during the day so I don't go off the deep end. Know what I mean?"

Then two things happened almost simultaneously. As the bartender walked away, Todd noticed he had both a red bulbous nose and splotchy red cheeks. Then he noticed the front door open and a mailman enter carrying a handful of mail. But it wasn't just any mailman. It was Bobby G., a member of Todd's home AA group and a man whose sobriety he really admired. He couldn't believe his eyes.

Bobby tossed the mail onto the bar. Then as he turned to leave, he spotted Todd at the end of the bar. He looked at Todd, shocked, and then walked quickly toward him and said rather loudly, "What the hell are you doing in here?"

"I don't know, Bobby," Todd replied, who was stunned by what was happening. "I guess I wanted to drink—but I didn't."

"Then why don't you get your ass out of here," the mailman said very firmly. "Why don't you just come with me."

When they walked back out into the street, Todd could hardly talk. By now he realized that God was doing for him what he couldn't do for himself. Then he saw that Bobby also appeared rather stunned, especially when he explained that Duffy's Tavern was not on his regular mail delivery route. He was filling in that day for a mail carrier who was on vacation.

After Todd pulled himself together, he called the executive recruiter and managed to postpone his interview until the following day. He then spent the rest of the afternoon walking with Bobby as he delivered his mail, listening to him talk about how something or somebody watches over alcoholics if they trust their Higher Power.

Four weeks later, Todd found a comfortable sales job at a smaller company. A year later, when he was ready to handle it, the Chicago executive recruiting firm placed him in an executive sales position with a much bigger company and at a much bigger salary. He and his wife reconciled. To this day, every time his mail arrives, Todd remembers the wonderful miracle God had his friend Bobby deliver and how it changed his entire life.

21
A Delayed Miracle

THE SOFT-SPOKEN PRIEST remembered that it was a lovely summer morning when the whole turbulent affair first began. As associate pastor of a missionary church in Southern California, Father Felix had just finished saying the 8:00 a.m. mass and was having breakfast in the church rectory when a good friend dropped by to ask a favor.

He was the Reverend Geraldo, director of Catholic Charities for the diocese, and he had been at the morning mass. It was there that he met a woman as he was leaving the church who had a special request. It seems her husband was dying, and she asked the priest if he would come to the hospital that day and give him the last rites of the church, also known as the anointing of the sick. He agreed.

Just as the woman left, Reverend Geraldo suddenly remembered he had to rush off to attend an important conference. So he came into the rectory and asked his friend Father Felix if he could perform the sacrament for him. His friend said it would be no problem, so he wrote down the woman's name, her husband's name, and the address and room number at the hospital.

However, at that moment, another pastor of the parish came in and overheard their conversation. It so happened that he was going in that direction and offered to give the dying man the last rites himself. Everyone was happy with the arrangement.

The pastor first went to lunch with some other friends in the clergy. He then completely forgot to stop at the hospital to tend to the dying man. That night the man passed away. His wife was furious that he did not receive the last rites, believing in her heart it was something her husband needed to enter heaven.

After the man's funeral, letters from the angry woman began flying everywhere—one to the pope, one to the apostolic delegate in Washington, D.C., one to the cardinal in Los Angeles, one to the local bishop, and finally one to the pastor of the missionary church who, unknown to the woman, had caused the ruckus in the first place.

The pastor was not the one she blamed. In the two-page inflammatory, condemning letter, she blamed everything on the priest she met in church that morning, the priest she believed had said the mass and promised to "save my husband's soul." She believed that priest was Father Felix and spelled his name out in capital letters throughout the angry missive.

After receiving the letter, the pastor sat down with his assistant and said in a rather embarrassed and regretful tone, "I know the woman asked Reverend Geraldo to go to the hospital, thinking he was you, and I agreed to do it instead. Then I simply forgot, and for some reason, you received the blame. Don't worry, Father. I will take care of it. I'll write to everyone and explain what happened and then talk with the woman myself."

Father Felix felt relieved. Weeks went by and nothing more was said. Then the young priest was stunned to learn that his superiors were still blaming him and were quite upset that nothing had been done to straighten out the matter. He approached his pastor, who refused to discuss it, saying it was a closed book. Deep inside Father Felix knew he had to at least try to clear things up with the angry woman and tell her he would offer several special masses for her late husband.

"I don't want to talk to you," the woman yelled into the phone when the young priest called. He tried to explain he was not the priest she spoke with that morning, but she kept insisting, "I know it was Father Felix who said the mass, and he was the one I told about my husband."

He calmly asked if she would come to the rectory to talk with his pastor and Reverend Geraldo to identify exactly who she spoke with so he could clear things up with his superiors, but she refused, saying, "I don't need to. I know it was Father Felix." Then she hung up.

A few months later, sometime around the end of May, the young priest was conducting a special ceremony in honor of the Blessed Virgin Mary. As he was leaving, someone who knew about the false accusations against him pointed to a woman in the crowd, saying that she was the one who wrote the disparaging letters. Father Felix approached her.

"Do you know who I am?" he asked the woman.

She looked at him with questioning eyes and shook her head.

"I'm Father Felix," he said.

The woman blushed, then turned and hurried away. And that's the way things stood for the next twenty-five years.

While the young priest was hurt and disappointed, he harbored no anger or bitterness in his heart. In fact, he would often pray for the woman and her late husband. It still bothered him, however, that his superiors had not completely exonerated him even after Reverend Geraldo gave testimony to the event.

Some years after the incident, he began serving as hospital chaplain at the community hospital. He did so for many years. Patients admitted to the facility were asked to note on their form if they had any religious preference. But those who came through the emergency room were not given that opportunity for some reason.

Father Felix, however, when making his priestly rounds, would always stop by the ER to see if any new patients had been admitted with life-threatening injuries or illnesses. One day as he was checking the list, he was shocked to see the name of the woman who said he had prevented her husband from going to heaven. He had forgiven but not forgotten. While it was twenty-five years later, it all came back to him as if it had just happened. And now, at the age of ninety-two, she had been admitted to the hospital with terminal cancer and needed a priest.

Father Felix walked into the woman's room unannounced. Her family was standing around her bedside and were pleased to see him. He looked down at the now elderly and sickly woman and asked, "Would you like to receive the last rites of the church?"

Suddenly the woman's faced filled with fear. Despite the many years that had passed, she recognized him. She turned her face away and began to cry. Father Felix stepped close, took her hand, and said, "Please don't be afraid. I've come to bring you God's peace, His love, and His forgiveness."

Slowly she turned toward him and as tears streamed down her face, she murmured, "Father, can you ever forgive me?"

He replied, "I did that a long time ago. So did our Heavenly Father."

The woman's daughter moved close and asked, "Are you Father Felix?"

He nodded.

"My mother told me so many times how she regretted doing what she did to you. She was so ashamed she just couldn't face you." Then the family stepped out into the hallway while the priest anointed the woman and heard her confession. When the family returned, the daughter remarked, "I've never seen my mother look so much at peace."

Later, after blessing the family and leaving the woman's hospital room, he knew deep inside that all that had happened was not a coincidence. He felt he was in the presence of God and knew that this was God's way of healing the wounds both he and the woman had carried for so long. Now they were both at peace.

"I know today," Father Felix says, "that I am a better priest for this experience. I have seen many miracles since, but none that I personally experienced changed my life as much as this one did."

22
Surrounded

HE HAD BEEN in and out of the rooms of Alcoholics Anonymous for more than eight years, never staying clean and sober for more than four or five months. And even then he wasn't really sober, just dry. So at the age of thirty-six, why he hadn't given up completely was something even Ray couldn't fathom.

He was a plumber by trade who lived near the docks in San Francisco. But his terrible addiction to alcohol and other drugs made it difficult for him to find and keep a good job. By now he was picking up any work he could around the docks to support his habit and pay the few bucks of rent at the squalid rooming house where he was surrounded by losers like himself. At least that's the way he looked at it.

The choice finally boiled down to either jumping off the docks and drowning himself or giving AA one last try. Ray decided on the latter and crawled back into a meeting one night with little hope that things would change. But God had other plans.

A man in his seventies whom everyone called "Paul the

Piano" stood next to the coffeepot watching Ray's hands tremble as he tried to fill his cup. Paul reached out, filled his cup for him, and led the somewhat unkempt young man to a chair down front.

Ray had known this thin, gray-haired man, once a great jazz pianist, since the first time he came to AA, but he didn't really like him. He thought he was a hard nose, a "Big Book thumper"—that either you do it his way or hit the highway. He always tried to avoid Paul and his type, but tonight he was willing to do anything that might help. So he followed the man to the front of the room, sat down next to him, and heard him say, "I'm glad to see you back, Ray. Like I've always told you, it's much easier to stay here than it is to come back. So this time, why not stay?"

For the next fifteen minutes before the meeting started, Paul the Piano shared with Ray how the disease of alcoholism wrecked his own career, how he struggled for more than a dozen years to get sober, and how he had to change his surroundings and leave all his sick cronies in the jazz business in order to have a chance at recovery from his disease. He then told Ray he'd be his temporary sponsor because he believed Ray really wanted to make it this time and he'd show him the way.

So, over the next three months, Ray made it to a meeting every night, tried to do everything Paul suggested, and even began asking every morning—rather uncomfortably at first— for God to help him stay sober. It wasn't too much of a struggle during the day and when he was with his sponsor each night. But it was a real battle when he'd return to that squalid rooming house and be surrounded by so many active alcoholics and drug addicts.

Paul kept telling his young friend he had to leave there, but where could he go without a steady job and the money to pay for a better place? He was getting desperate. One night at the rooming house, a drunk stuck a half-pint of booze in his face, daring him to drink it. Ray ran into his room, got down on his knees, and begged God to get him out of there.

The very next night, as he walked into the AA meeting, Marty, a retired electrician from Los Angeles, pulled him aside. He said he had a good friend in the commercial plumbing business in L.A. who was looking for help. He wanted to know if Ray would be willing to move there. Just then Paul the Piano approached, noticed the shocked look on his young friend's face, and asked what was wrong. Ray asked Marty to repeat what he had just said. Then his wise old sponsor smiled.

"When God thinks we're ready, son," he said, "He offers us opportunities. I understand there are great AA meetings in Los Angeles. So why not accept Marty's offer? It's probably God's offer too."

A week later, Ray found himself driving his beat-up ten-year-old Pontiac into the parking lot of a large Los Angeles plumbing contractor. He was surprised to see a bumper sticker on a brand-new Cadillac parked near the office that read, "Honk if you know Bill W." He smiled as a comfortable feeling ran through him.

He was even more surprised when he entered the office and discovered that the Cadillac belonged to Richie, the owner of the plumbing company. Marty back in San Francisco hadn't told him Richie was in AA, too, because he believed in the tradition of not breaking anyone's anonymity.

All these so-called coincidences were simply part of the quiet miracle God was performing in the life of this plumber who had finally become willing to do anything to stay sober. And more was yet to come.

Richie, the owner, told Ray he had rented him a furnished studio apartment in a small, well-kept apartment house in nearby Woodland Hills. Ray drove out with his few belongings and settled in. That afternoon, he was watching TV when there was a knock on his door. He opened it to find the sober faces of two men about his age grinning at him.

One was Arnie and the other Sid. They had come at Richie's request to take him to an AA meeting. Ray's eyes moistened, knowing this was all the work of his Higher Power. On the way to the meeting, Ray happened to mention how great his new digs were compared with the squalid rooming house back in San Francisco and the tenants that populated it. Arnie and Sid started to laugh. Then they told their AA friend that not only did they also live at the Woodland Hills apartment house, but that twenty-two of the thirty-five apartments were occupied by sober members of AA.

Where once Ray was surrounded by drunks and drug addicts, now he was surrounded by recovering alcoholics. It proved to him once again what Paul the Piano had always said, that God will do for us what we cannot do for ourselves.

23
Her Hate Melted Away

ROBIN STARED INTO the bathroom mirror and began to cry. She was only twenty-nine, yet the pale, blotchy face staring back at her through red eyes and kinky, matted hair seemed so much older.

Twelve years of alcoholic drinking and popping pills had changed her from a happy, carefree young woman who used to love romping across the beaches in San Diego to an angry, slovenly, hermitlike person who now sat alone in her filthy apartment, hating the world and everyone in it.

She wanted to break the bathroom mirror. Instead, she staggered back into the living room to take another swig from the vodka bottle. As the warm liquid ran down her throat, she knew she couldn't go on like this. It wasn't only her fears and anxieties that made her drink more and more, it was also all those seething, painful resentments that were eating her alive. It seemed as if they were with her all the time now.

Robin hated her younger sister, Lorrie. She felt she was a

spoiled brat who was given far more than Robin had ever received. She hated her father for spoiling Lorrie, handing her anything she wanted while depriving Robin of the attention she craved. That's the way she saw it, and every drink she took convinced her it was true.

And then there was her alcoholic mother, who was never there when she needed her. She was either drunk in some bar or passed out in bed. After a while her father couldn't stand it anymore, so he left. In fact, he snuck off one night without ever saying good-bye to Robin and her sister.

But when it came to huge, burning resentments, that one she saved for Kathy, who had been her closest and dearest friend ever since they first sat next to each other in kindergarten. They were inseparable growing up, even getting drunk together one night as teenagers. By their senior year in high school, however, they had begun to drift apart.

While also a heavy drinker, Kathy managed to get it under control and went off to college. She made it through and came out with a degree in computer science. Robin, on the other hand, entered the work world and continued to drink. She wound up managing the dress department in a large, upscale department store where she met, dated, and fell in love with the owner's handsome son, Cameron. He liked to party, too, and had plenty of money to do it.

Robin attended Kathy's college graduation and brought her boyfriend along. She should have sensed something was going amiss when Cameron congratulated Kathy by giving her a long, amorous hug. But because Robin was already a little high on gin and tonics and had faith in Kathy and in her date, her perception was clouded. She didn't see or suspect what was coming.

Cameron suddenly ended his relationship with Robin and started dating her once closest and dearest friend. She was devastated. She went into a tailspin, drinking more than ever and popping more pills. When Kathy married Cameron some months later, Robin hit bottom.

She could no longer work at the department store. There were too many painful memories. So she went to work in a small dress shop. She soon lost that job because of her drinking. When she had been doing well, she purchased a one-bedroom condo in a nice area of San Diego. That went too. She moved into a small studio apartment in a not-so-nice area and began bouncing from job to job just to pay the rent and buy booze.

Robin hadn't seen Kathy in several years, but she was never out of her mind. This morning her hatred for her former friend was almost unbearable. She sat on the couch and finished the vodka, but this time it didn't take away the pain. What was she going to do? Robin knew she needed help, but what kind of help? Should she call the few friends she had left to borrow some money for more vodka and pills, or should she go to the hospital to dry out in the detox ward to get her mind working right again?

That's when she suddenly remembered the phone call she received from her mother a few nights ago. Robin didn't want to talk to her. She still hated her mother. However, she had been sending her daughter a few bucks now and then, so she forced herself to listen to her usual sad tales. Only this time it was different.

Her mother said she had finally decided to join Alcoholics Anonymous and had been sober a few months. It was working. She hadn't felt this good and this hopeful in years. But as she began talking about the meetings she was attending and the wonderful people she was meeting, Robin sensed her mother was about to preach to her about the evils of drink. She couldn't listen to such hypocrisy, so she hung up.

She angrily threw the empty vodka bottle across the room and walked to the window. As she stared out, an intriguing thought occurred to her: *Why don't I call my mother back right now and tell her how sick I am? She'll put me in the hospital and pay all the bills and my rent too because she owes me at least that much. Then in a few weeks I'll feel better, get a new job, and everything will be just fine.* That's the way Robin always liked it—the easier, softer way.

When she got her mother on the phone and moaned about how sick she was, Robin expected instant sympathy and an immediate offer of help. She anticipated her mother would dash over to her apartment with a big, fat check to pay for all her needs. That's not what happened.

Instead, in a very calm, unemotional voice, she told her daughter she should hang up and immediately call the Intergroup Office of AA. She should tell whoever answers that she has a serious drinking problem and wants help. Her mother assured her they would send someone over to her apartment to take her to an AA meeting. She said that's what she did, and it worked for her.

Robin slammed down the phone. She couldn't believe what she had just heard—but why should she be surprised at a mother who never cared for her growing up refusing to care for her now when she was in such great need. She began pacing back and forth, cursing and condemning everyone in her life for not caring, for their lack of understanding, for not doing anything to help her. Then she slumped back down into the couch and began crying. She was lost, hopeless. All she could think of saying was "God, please help me. I don't know what to do."

The words had barely left her lips when she seemed to hear her mother's quiet, calm voice saying to her, "Call them. It worked for me. It can work for you."

For some reason she reached over, picked up the phone book, and looked up the number of the AA Intergroup Office. She dialed. A man answered with a very kind voice. He took her name and address and said a woman would be by to see her in a few hours. Robin went into the bathroom and took a shower. She brushed her hair, put on something comfortable, then sat with a cup of tea in her shaking hands and waited.

The doorbell rang. She opened the door and couldn't believe who was standing there. It was Kathy, her once closest and dearest friend. Robin was stunned. Her head was spinning. She wanted to slam the door in her face, but something told her not to. Then she heard Kathy say, "Hi, Robin. It's Kathy, and I'm an alcoholic too. I came because you called. I'm sorry about all that has happened. Can we talk?"

Robin nodded, still too shocked and confused to speak. Kathy entered and sat on the couch. Robin sat across from her.

She listened as her once most-hated friend explained how she had lost everything through her drinking—her marriage, her home, her friends, and her health. She joined AA two years ago. She had tried to find Robin to make amends but was unable to until now.

Recently she had been volunteering at AA's Intergroup Office to make Twelve Step calls to women like herself to help them find sobriety. She just happened to be there when Robin called. They both knew it was no coincidence, that it was one of God's quiet miracles. They stood and hugged for a long time as Robin's hatred and resentment toward Kathy melted away.

Today their friendship is stronger than it ever was, and it continues to grow in sobriety and through the miracle God worked in their lives.

24
Expired in the Nick of Time

FIRST THEY WOULD have dinner at their favorite seafood restaurant near the pier. Then they would take an exciting evening cruise off the Carolina coast on a festive gambling ship. No, they couldn't afford it, but Spence insisted that his wife, Valerie, deserved it for being such a "good girl" these past few months.

What he really meant was that his wife had been sober since Valentine's Day, and now that it was close to the Fourth of July—it was about time they celebrated. Valerie would have preferred dinner at a small buffet followed by a movie, but her husband insisted that they "break out and live a little."

Spence couldn't understand his wife's hesitation about having a night on the town, to dine and dance and have fun like they used to do—that is, before her heavy drinking became such a serious problem. But now she had it "under control," and if it was spending money they didn't have that concerned her, he said he'd work overtime to make it up.

It wasn't really the money as far as his wife was concerned. Certainly they were deeply in debt from all she had spent on alcohol and other drugs in addition to her husband's long layoff from work. But his company had recently called him back, and she had found a job at a large retail chain. So while the future looked a little brighter, she still had those other fears inside her.

It was mainly that her husband didn't understand her concerns about being around alcohol and a partying crowd. After six months of sobriety in the program of Alcoholics Anonymous, Valerie was just beginning to lose her desire to drink and gain the ability to meet life on life's terms as a sober woman. Her husband, however, still thought it was a matter of willpower. After all, he drank quite a bit and never made a fool out of himself like his wife used to do.

But he was happy that things were different now. She was taking good care of their two children, shopping, keeping the house clean, and even bringing home a few bucks. He felt she deserved to relax and have some fun.

Since Valerie couldn't change her husband's plans without starting another argument—something she wanted to avoid at all costs now that there was some harmony at home—she kept telling herself it would be a wonderful evening. She would carry the Serenity Prayer in her purse to say if she ran into a problem. She could also take a long walk on the ship's deck if there was too much drinking and revelry going on around her.

The night started out far better than she expected. They arrived at the restaurant around 6:00 p.m. and sat near the large picture windows that overlooked the harbor and a marina filled with stately sailboats and luxury yachts. Since the gambling ship was close by and didn't depart until 8:00 p.m., they had plenty of time to relax and enjoy dinner. There was even enough time for a few dances to the music of a local trio. It was the first dance that did it.

The insidious disease of alcoholism always paints a past filled with soft lights and moonglow, the delightful tinkling of cocktail glasses and the warmth of liquor on the palate, the gentle movements on a dance floor, and a lover's intimate embrace. Valerie was no exception to the mental magnetism of booze.

As her husband led her onto the dance floor, she started to feel awkward and clumsy. Her body seemed to stiffen, and her legs turned to wood. She didn't have those few drinks that would always turn her into a Broadway performer or a Hollywood coquette, those few drinks that made the lights a little brighter and the music a little sweeter, those few drinks that turned a dark and dreary world into an exciting whirlwind of sheer exhilaration.

And when she sat at the table to enjoy her favorite steak and lobster dinner, it didn't taste the same. A few glasses of wine always seemed to bring out the flavor and make the food go down easier. And then she would look forward to the rum cake and coffee laced with brandy to top things off.

As Valerie glanced across to a nearby table, where a waiter was filling wineglasses for an obviously happy couple, she suddenly made up her mind that she wasn't going to ruin this evening for her husband. She wasn't going to be a wet blanket and dampen all his fun. She intended to loosen up—to eat and dance and gamble and laugh and have fun like they used to do back then. And to get into the mood, she decided she'd sneak off once they got on the ship and have a few drinks— just a few to loosen up.

But when they finished dinner and walked from the restaurant, Valerie began struggling with the demons in her head. She didn't want to drink, but she knew she was going to once she got on board. She knew what might happen, but she had already made up her mind to drink and nothing was going to stop her. Certainly she would try to control her drinking so as not to upset her husband, but she was still going to drink regardless.

The pier where the brilliantly lit and gaily decorated gambling ship was docked was only a short distance away. Spence already had quite a bit to drink at dinner and was in an excited and festive mood. He was laughing loudly and happily as he pulled his wife through the crowd to get there faster. When they finally arrived at the gated entrance, there were two uniformed men checking photo IDs.

Valerie approached one of the uniformed men, opened her purse, and handed him her driver's license with her picture on it. He checked it, smiled, and handed it back. She walked a few steps onto the pier before turning back to locate her husband. She was surprised to see him still at the entrance gate, arguing with the other uniformed man. She walked over and approached them.

Valerie was shocked when she saw what was taking place. She knew at once that what was happening was no mere coincidence. Tears filled her eyes as she realized that there was a Power greater than herself doing something for her at this very moment that she could not do for herself.

Spence's driver's license had expired. Angry and depressed over being laid off from his job, he had forgotten to get it renewed. Because of rigid security regulations, the man at the gate could not accept an invalid driver's license. As a result, he would not let Spence onto the gambling ship.

Her husband was irate. Valerie pretended to be upset too, but deep inside she felt enormous relief. As they walked slowly from the pier, she realized that her desire for a drink had left and in its place was a warm feeling of gratitude.

Spence was too angry to go to a movie. He decided simply to go home and have a few more drinks. He dropped his wife off at an AA meeting along the way.

To this day, when Valerie looks at her driver's license, she remembers how her Higher Power kept her sober that night through a quiet, little miracle that changed the whole rest of her life.

25
And Lead Us Not into Temptation

JACK HAD OFTEN heard from some of his more religious friends that saying the Lord's Prayer every day is like paying the premium on an insurance policy you might need for some future crisis. He didn't really believe it. Today he does.

It all came about during a business trip to Frankfurt, Germany, one cold and blustery week in December. As a sales representative for a large American industrial products company, he had spent the week meeting with the company's sales agents in and around the city as well as trying to line up some new reps elsewhere. The weather was foul, and his meetings didn't go as well as he had hoped. So, on the last day of his trip, he decided to stay at an inexpensive hotel near Frankfurt's central train station so he could simply ride the train out to the airport the next day.

That evening he set out on foot to explore that part of the city as well as to get something to eat and drink. There was a winter festival in town where he thought he might enjoy some hot mulled wine, something his father used to make each Christmas until he passed away a few months ago.

Jack soon realized, however, that he had started out in the wrong direction. It turned out that his hotel was within one block of Frankfurt's red light district. This area was made up of several older hotels that were converted into brothels and had women on display in nearly every room and in the hotel windows. The industrial products salesman was more than a bit intrigued. He had spent several protective years in a seminary studying to be a minister before leaving. He married a short time later, so he had never really seen anything like this before—at least not on such a grand scale.

The flesh was all too willing that night and the spirit terribly weak for several reasons. First was the pressure on him to meet his sales quota, and it wasn't going well. Second, before leaving his hotel, he had spoken to his wife on the phone, and they had gotten into a tiff over their teenage daughter, one of their four children. And then the bad weather on top of it all put him in a very down mood. Maybe what he needed was a little fun. At least that's what the demons in his head were telling him.

So, without giving it too much thought at first, he began walking from one brothel to another, up and down the hotel stairways, checking out each and every scantily clad prostitute displaying her physical attributes. It was as if he were window-shopping before deciding to make a purchase.

The more he looked, the more the temptation grew. Jack knew he had enough money to "close a deal" with one of these women. But he also knew there wouldn't be enough left for a good dinner and some gifts he planned to purchase to bring home to his family for the holidays—mainly a new winter coat for his wife.

It was only when he saw a young, attractive dark-haired girl smiling at him—a girl that reminded him of his teen-age daughter—that he snapped out of his wanton trance. He suddenly realized he was being drawn into doing something that could have serious consequences. Not only would he be cheating on his wife and have to live with that guilt, but he could wind up with AIDS or another sexually transmitted disease. Still, he couldn't rid himself of the tempting delights before him.

Since he had not yet settled on one particular woman, Jack decided to take a brief respite from his "shopping tour" and continue his walk. He knew the attractive menu would still be there upon his return.

There was a main thoroughfare two blocks away lined with fine restaurants and a variety of shops, including several clothing stores. As he approached, he noticed a lot of commotion on one street corner. He walked over and dis-covered that a coat store was having an impromptu sidewalk sale. There was a display of lovely winter coats with beautiful fur collars on one particular rack—just the kind of coat he was thinking of buying for his wife for Christmas.

As Jack stood there staring at the coatrack, he felt God stepping back into his life. He was being given the choice of spending his money on a coat for his wife or on a few mo-ments of questionable pleasure with a prostitute. The choice became that simple. He reached out, took a fur-collared coat from the rack, and entered the store.

One of the sales staff inside appeared to be about the same size as his wife. The coat fit her perfectly. As he reached into his pocket for his money, the demons struck again. He thought about all those beautiful women and said to himself, *I can charge this coat on my credit card and still have the cash to go back to the brothel.*

But the God Jack prayed the Lord's Prayer to every morning on his knees stepped in to help him once again. As he handed the saleswoman his credit card, she told him, "I'm sorry, sir. This coat is on sale, so you must pay for it in cash. We won't accept a credit card."

Jack's knees buckled. He could feel the hand of God delivering him from evil once again. Even though he knew he had already committed lust in his heart, God was sparing him from all the other possible consequences that could have ensued had he returned to the brothel. His eyes were moist as he counted out the money for his wife's new coat, a gift he could now give her with a clear conscience.

Jack spent what was left of his money on some bread, meat, cheese, and a small bottle of apple cider. Then he went back to his hotel and called his wife to express his love for her and his family. As he flew home the next day, he thought about how he had been tempted beyond his own spiritual strength, yet he prevailed because God performed a quiet miracle in his life.

Jack's story has an interesting postscript. When he arrived back in his office the following Monday, he had inquiries from three potential new sales agents in Germany and substantial orders from two of his largest customers in Frankfurt. Maybe this was God's way of saying all is forgiven.

26
It Happened in a Car Wash

By the time she had eked her way through college and entered what she considered an often harsh and challenging world, "self-reliance" had become Marie's stalwart mantra. And even though she believed in God, her strong self-will frequently found her arguing with her Creator over almost every aspect of her life. So by the time she was in her late forties, she had stopped asking God for anything. Why should she when it felt like every single prayer she said was answered by a resounding "no"?

Yes, Marie would admit she felt sorry for herself at times, but then who wouldn't? Her marriage was coming apart, her three children rarely called or wrote anymore, and her nursing career—the only thing she seemed to care about—was apparently over after another episode of messing up a patient's medications.

And now, three months later, she was sitting in her bedroom, once again drinking blueberry brandy and staring out the window into a gray winter sky. Her perfectionism in the art of self-deception was still telling her that blueberry brandy is good for a cold, and it seems like she's been nursing an eternal cold. Actually, that's how Marie had been denying her alcoholism for so many years—justifying why she drank and how much she drank.

At first it was just to have a little fun and loosen up, something she couldn't seem to do without a few drinks. Then it was the pressure from her job and the need to relax after work. When her husband, Frank, began to notice her heavy drinking, the arguments started. In Marie's alcoholic mind, her husband was being unkind, dogmatic, and unloving and was showing a complete lack of understanding. When you have a husband like that to blame, it can justify a multitude of drinks. It can also wreck a marriage, which it was now doing.

Frank was spending more time staying at the downtown athletic club than he was at home. And if he was showing a lack of understanding, his wife was showing it even more. She couldn't see that her husband still loved her but was completely lost and frustrated by her drinking. He wanted to help but was rejected at every turn. In fact, he even went to a few Al-Anon meetings in the city trying to comprehend why his wife seemed to be throwing away everything that was near and dear to her.

One day as Marie staggered from her bedroom to replenish her booze supply, she tripped and fell down the stairs, breaking her arm and wrenching her neck. Her sister, who lived nearby, took her to the hospital emergency room for treatment—the same hospital where she had last worked.

The doctor who tended her that day was an old friend who had talked with her on several occasions about her drinking. However, after being rather harshly rebuffed, he simply backed off and said no more. This time, seeing the shape Marie was in, he decided to speak with her again—lovingly but firmly. He strongly suggested she attend some meetings of Alcoholics Anonymous. He even gave her the name and phone number of a woman in the program. The woman happened to be his wife.

Marie was greatly taken that the doctor would go to such lengths to help her and was also impressed that his wife was a member of AA. She promised to call as soon as she got home. She also promised to keep the doctor's secret just as she wanted no one to find out about her drinking. The doctor smiled. Familiar with the problem, he understood.

So Marie finally put the cork in her blueberry brandy bottle and began attending AA meetings. The doctor's wife became her sponsor. Despite her broken arm and sore neck, she went to meetings every night with her sponsor, who quickly got her into the program's Twelve Steps of recovery. Things went fine until they reached the Third Step: "Made a decision to turn our will and our lives over to the care of God *as we understood Him.*"

The problem was that Marie and God were still on the "outs." How do you turn your life and your will over to the care of someone you're still angry with for not helping you all these years? And, she thought, if God wouldn't help her with her problems in the past, why would He do so now when she was even less deserving of His help? Even after many conversations with her sponsor and reading about the Third Step in AA's Big Book, Marie was still confused. She couldn't seem to figure out how or where to begin taking this important spiritual step.

In the meantime, Marie's arm mended, the soreness left her neck, and most important, she and Frank reconciled. She had also gotten a new nursing job at a small health clinic some distance from her home. She was happy to be back in the profession she loved so much. However, the long drive to and from the clinic together with her AA meetings had her on a tight schedule. She found little time to keep her car clean, which bothered her.

One day as she stopped for a red light while driving home from work, she noticed an automatic car wash across the way. On impulse, she drove her rather dirty car up to the front entrance and looked around for someone to direct her. She had never been to an automatic car wash before, so she didn't know what to do.

Then two young men appeared at the front entrance. One approached and said the charge would be eight dollars. She paid while the other young man quickly hosed off her car's front and rear wheels. Then they both disappeared. After a few moments when they didn't return, Marie began to feel uneasy. She suspected she was supposed to do something, but what? Then the guy in the car behind her began honking his horn, blasting her into action.

She could see water streaming down in front of her inside the car wash. So she began to drive forward. Gigantic brushes whirled against her windshield, and soapy white foam oblit-erated her vision. She couldn't see ahead, behind, or to the sides. Disregarding the bumps, clangs, and squeals, the now very nervous nurse continued to drive straight ahead, emerging into the bright sunlight with suds dripping from the car and perspiration pouring off her brow.

One of the young men was standing in front of her car shaking his head in total disbelief.

"Go around again, lady," he shouted, "and read the signs."

Marie whispered, "Okay," as she felt the need to surrender to his directions.

Reaching the front entrance once again, the other young man slowly guided her into putting the two front wheels of her car on the track. Then he pointed to the large sign hanging over the entrance to the car wash. It read:

PUT YOUR CAR IN NEUTRAL.
TAKE YOUR HANDS OFF THE WHEEL.
TAKE YOUR FOOT OFF THE BRAKE.

Then the young man leaned his head into her open window and told her emphatically, "Just remember, lady, don't drive it. And for God's sake, just let go of the steering wheel!"

Marie rolled up her car window with renewed confidence. Now the machinery that she didn't understand was no longer frightening. She had gained, through surrender, new eyes to see with and new ears to hear with. She was led through the washing, waxing, and rinsing, and it was all okay as she let go and let it happen.

This time the humbled nurse coasted out into the sunlight with her car shining and her face beaming. For here at this car wash, Marie not only had two car washes for the price of one, but she knew in her very soul that God had shown her how to draw close and trust Him through the Third Step.

That day at the automatic car wash created a major change in Marie's way of life. She began to turn everything over to the care of her Higher Power—her marriage, her children, her nursing career. She has not taken it back since.

27
An Apt Salute to Fifty Sober Years

THE DAY KIRK celebrated his first year of sobriety in the fellowship of Alcoholics Anonymous, he received a call from his grandfather in Connecticut to congratulate him. That was the first nice surprise. The second was his grandfather's revelation that he was also a member of AA and had gone almost fifty years without a drink. He said he knew Kirk could do the same or better starting out at such a young age.

Kirk had just turned twenty-six. He had always looked up to his grandfather, a strong, quiet man he loved to visit as a youngster. But it wasn't as often as he would have liked since his parents lived some distance away in another state. And then as a young man, his drinking and partying became more important than visiting relatives. When he was thrown out of college for drinking, he became too ashamed to see anyone.

Kirk never knew his grandfather had a problem with alcohol and attended AA. He had kept it to himself all these years, and no one in the family ever mentioned it. At least Kirk had never heard about it. Perhaps his family respected the anonymity of the AA fellowship. So the call from his grandfather made the young man feel proud that they were in the same program together, and it bolstered his determination to stay sober.

He found it a joy to travel to Connecticut and once again visit his grandfather. It was an even greater joy to go with him to a few AA meetings. They became close once again. However, by the time Kirk's second sober anniversary rolled around, his grandfather had gotten ill and was hospitalized. No one told Kirk how serious the illness was, so by the time he arranged to take a few days off from work to visit him in the hospital, his grandfather had already passed away.

The news hit Kirk hard. In fact, he thought for a moment about having a drink. Instead, he did all the things he knew his grandfather would have suggested he do in sad and difficult circumstances: talk with his sponsor, go to a meeting, and don't drink. He stayed sober, but it didn't relieve the pain and disappointment.

Kirk made arrangements to be there for his grandfather's funeral. His parents, other relatives, and friends—mostly AA members—would also be there. It was scheduled for Good Friday, not the nicest time of year in Connecticut. The young man felt intense grief the morning he saw his grandfather for the last time at the funeral home. He was surprised to learn there would be no church service. Instead, they would all follow the hearse to a small country cemetery some fifteen miles away, near the town where his grandfather was born.

As they were approaching the gates of the cemetery, Kirk recalled that this day would have been his grandfather's fiftieth anniversary of sobriety in AA. He hoped there might be someone at the graveside to recognize that fact, some salute to this wonderful man's great achievement—living a good and sober life for half a century. But there was no one, not even a preacher. He waited in silence, hoping one of the AA members there would step forward. But no one did.

Then Kirk's father approached him. He handed him a prayer book. He said the family all agreed that since he and his grandfather had grown so close and had so much in common, they would like him to conduct a small service. It wasn't that Kirk was afraid to talk in front of people. He had done that many times at AA meetings. It was just that he was hoping for more—for some special recognition for this kind, loving, and sober man. He felt inadequate to do that.

As everyone waited quietly and uncomfortably in the chilly morning air, Kirk opened the prayer book and nervously recited a few prayers for the dead. Then he commented about how proud he was of his grandfather, how much he loved him, and how he deserved a much greater salute for his accomplishments than his poor words could achieve. To close, he asked if everyone would hold hands and recite the Lord's Prayer, thinking that's how his grandfather would like the brief service to end.

Just as everyone was ending the prayer with a strong "Amen," the steeple bells in the small, white church next to the cemetery began to ring out as if as on cue. Kirk looked at his watch. It was 11:40 a.m., an odd time for church bells to start ringing. But as the bells continued to peal, the sun suddenly broke through the clouds. It was a perfect ending to the funeral service and an apt salute to fifty years of sobriety.

It was also appropriate since his grandfather was a collector of chiming clocks, and now these church bells were chiming him a final farewell.

When he was leaving the cemetery, Kirk approached the funeral director and asked how he managed to have the church bells rung so precisely at the end of their closing prayer. The funeral director looked perplexed. Kirk was shocked when he replied that the church bells had been inoperative for years, and he couldn't explain what happened. That's when Kirk knew that God had done something for his grandfather that he was unable to do.

Later that day the young man discovered that the elders at the little white church had only recently raised enough money to have the bells repaired. They were being tested at 11:40 that morning. That didn't change what Kirk knew in his heart—that this was all another gift from his Higher Power because God had already proved to him many times that He often works in very strange and mysterious ways.

28
No Angry Good-byes

FOR MORE THAN thirty years, Jerome worked as a nursing home administrator, serving primarily at geriatric and psychiatric facilities, caring for the poor and indigent. It was for the most part a tedious and thankless job but one that sometimes gave him great personal satisfaction.

This kind and dedicated man often said it was impossible to work in this field with such a caring staff and not see beyond the physical to the spiritual. However, he believed the sadness and suffering could dull one's senses if you let them—and the work could become like watching the sun rise and set without being awed by God's majesty.

There was one particular little miracle Jerome never forgot that involved a seriously ill elderly lady who made a great impact on his life. He had just taken a new job as administrator of a rural sixty-bed geriatric center where everyone knew each other quite well, staff and residents alike. It was a small, homelike facility where the rooms were filled with personal effects and families visited often—that is, with one exception. Her name was Mary, an elderly woman whose angry tongue and vile words everyone tried to ignore. But it wasn't easy. She was also the only one at the nursing home who never had any visitors.

The day Jerome arrived at the facility to take on his new job, he couldn't help but notice two things. First, the place appeared as old and as poor as the dying town nearby. The screen door squeaked, the front door was painted a sickly reddish brown, and the entrance hall was dimly lit. The second thing he noticed was Mary seated in her basic generic wheelchair just inside the front entrance. The eighty-nine-year-old lady weighed less than eighty pounds. Her snowy white hair was in disarray, and her red, bloodshot eyes stared angrily in his direction.

As the new administrator approached her, Mary's thin, bony finger shot into the air, and she began spitting and screaming obscenities in his direction. Strangely, Jerome was not repulsed, which would have been the reaction of most. Instead, he was attracted by the almost pleading anger in her voice and the sadness in her eyes.

At first he thought this lady may have been mistreated or not well cared for because he knew that such behavior on the part of a patient can attract the same kind of behavior in return. He soon learned this wasn't the case. She was simply a difficult person to deal with since the day she arrived at the nursing facility.

At his first staff meeting that morning, the new administrator told everyone that Mary was going to be his favorite resident. He said he would like her to receive especially warm and loving care. However, if anyone found that too difficult because of her attitude and actions, he would certainly understand and not hold it against them. He would simply assign another staff person to attend her.

Jerome quickly learned that his expressed desire was not going to be easy to achieve. Mary was very stubborn and obstinate and difficult to bathe, feed, or assist in any way—even to ease her extreme arthritic pain. For a whole year the administrator went out of his way to personally treat Mary with all the respect and dignity human beings deserve and certainly far more than her actions called for. And he was fully supportive of his staff and all the frustrations and challenges they continually faced with Mary and the other patients— challenges that society does not generally understand or appreciate.

Every now and then the administrator thought he sensed a slight change in the elderly lady's demeanor. However, when he would try to engage her in polite conversation, she would refuse to reply or speak with him. But he could see that the really vile attacks were lessening as the days, weeks, and months went by.

Then one day Heddy, Jerome's certified nursing assistant, came running into his office. There were tears in her eyes as she blurted out, "Jerome! She's asking to see you. Mary is asking to see Jerome!"

The administrator rose from behind his desk with a deep frown on his forehead. "That can't be," he replied. "I don't believe Mary even knows my name. She never asked for it, and she certainly never used it. In fact, I have never heard Mary speak except for that angry profanity, which never makes any sense."

"But she keeps asking to see Jerome," the nurse insisted as she wiped her tears away. "Please come with me right away."

As he followed Heddy quickly down the hallway, Jerome sensed something out of the ordinary was happening. Upon entering Mary's room, he saw her sitting up in bed pointing toward the door and saying rather loudly and very clearly, "I keep telling you, I want to see Jerome."

The stunned administrator slowly approached the bed. The once difficult and angry patient smiled at him and said very lovingly, "Jerome. There you are. Please, come a little closer. I have to tell you something."

Jerome hesitated for just a moment, still fully aware of Mary's ability to suddenly lash out. But never had he heard her speak in such a kind and loving manner. He moved closer. His eyes were mesmerized by hers. Those once red and blood-shot eyes were now a beautiful, shiny blue. The sadness was gone, as if the terrible pain and suffering that controlled her was now also gone. He stood at her bedside.

"Jerome," she smiled. "I want to thank you for all the kindness and respect you showed to this nasty, old lady. I am deeply grateful to you for making me feel wanted—for making me feel loved. I needed to see you so I could tell you that. Now I want to say good-bye."

The deeply touched administrator reached out to take her tiny hand into his. He started to chide her for even suggesting she was leaving them. She cast his hand aside as if to rebuke him for not appreciating the moment. Then she gently grasped it again, smiled warmly, and whispered, "Thank you, Jerome."

Then Mary took her final breath and passed away. Jerome can still remember feeling her soul leave her body. He has never feared death since that day. That was the last and greatest gift Mary gave him as a reward for his kindness and respect. Jerome also knew it was another one of God's quiet miracles.

29
God Sent Her a State Trooper

SHE HAD HEARD her husband, Paul, threaten to divorce her a thousand times before. Only this time, as she stood in her kitchen swaying from too many glasses of wine, Rose watched as he waved the actual divorce papers in front of her. It was something she could no longer ignore, pretend wasn't happening, walk away from, or feign sorrow and remorse over as she had done so many times before.

This time there was a determined look on her husband's face and an angry glare in his eyes, a glare that aroused well-justified guilt in her alcoholic soul. As she turned back toward the kitchen counter and began pouring herself another glass of wine, Paul grabbed it from her hand and threw it into the sink.

"You can have all the damn drinks you want after you sign these papers!" he shouted at her. "This time I come first, not your damn booze."

Rose slumped into a kitchen chair. Paul threw the papers in front of her, handed her a pen, and pointed to the space for her signature. Her hand trembled as she scribbled her name on two copies. Then her husband yanked the documents from the table and stormed out of the kitchen. After a few moments, she heard the front door slam as he left the house.

The thin, dark-haired mother of three didn't remember anything else until she awoke the next morning on the couch. An empty wine bottle was next to her on the floor. She had apparently continued drinking after her husband left and went into a blackout. Her blackouts were occurring more frequently of late. Only last month she woke up in a motel room next to some man she had never seen before, at least as far as she could recall. It filled her with guilt and remorse.

Rose knew in her heart this couldn't continue, but she had no idea she had a disease that made her powerless over alcohol. She only knew she wanted to stop drinking and everything that went with it, but as hard as she tried, she just couldn't quit.

For the last five years her husband had been telling her she needed help. Her two older daughters would plead with her to go to an alcohol rehab. But the strong, self-willed woman kept insisting she could stop—or at least cut back—on her own. Her younger son never said a word, probably because he had as big or bigger problems with alcohol and other drugs than his mother.

Rose finally managed to push herself off the couch and stagger back into the kitchen. A copy of the divorce papers was still there on the table. That's when it all came back to her. She leaned against the counter and began to weep. Then she heard a voice deep down inside her saying, *This is the end of the line. You either do something or you will die.*

She opened a drawer in the counter and took out the Yellow Pages phone book. She thumbed through it until she found the listing for alcohol rehabilitation centers. One of them had a half-page ad that read "Hope, Help, and Recovery." As she stared at it, a sparkle of hope began generating inside her. She called, gave them the information they needed, and was told to come right away before she changed her mind. She promised she would and wrote down the directions. It was about thirty miles away.

Determined not to let anything stand in her way, Rose hurried upstairs, took a quick shower, dressed, and packed a small suitcase. Then she went back downstairs and checked the house before leaving. As she walked back into the kitchen, she began shaking and perspiring. She sat down in a chair to calm down.

"I'm definitely going," she kept telling herself. "But I don't think I can make it like this. Maybe I'll just have a few drinks to settle my nerves and then I'll be off."

It made perfectly good sense to this bewildered and frightened alcoholic since she was now so determined to get help. But to reach the place to get that help, she felt she would have to get rid of the shakes and calm her nerves. She was certain just a few drinks would do it. So she reached down and pulled out a full bottle of wine from behind a stack of pots and pans. She opened it, filled a tall glass, and sipped it very slowly since she was certain this would be her very last drink. But it took the second glass to calm her nerves and the third to take away the shakes.

The next thing Rose recalled was a loud pounding on a door. She was coming out of another blackout curled up on the filthy floor of a gas station restroom. The next sound she heard was an authoritative man's voice on the other side of the door saying, "I'm State Trooper Johnson, ma'am, and I need for you to come out of the restroom. Please do so right away."

Rose managed to get to her feet, straighten out her clothes, and throw some cold water on her face. Then she staggered out into the blazing sunlight to see the angry face of a tall state trooper staring down at her. He said he spotted her speeding and weaving all over the interstate but was unable to stop her despite his blaring siren until she drove into the gas station and staggered into the restroom.

"May I ask where you were going in such a hurry, and in such a condition?" the trooper demanded to know.

The pale, red-eyed lady lowered her head and nervously mumbled, "I'm on my way to an alcohol rehab center. I have a terrible drinking problem, and I'm going to get help."

Trooper Johnson was taken aback at first, but then he shook his head, for it made all the sense in the world, particularly seeing her disheveled look and smelling the wine on her breath. The angry look left his face and was replaced with a kind, understanding smile.

"I'll tell you what, ma'am," the trooper said. "You tell me where that rehab is located, and I'll be happy to drive you there. We can leave your car parked here, and I'll have someone take it there tomorrow."

Rose began to cry. As clouded as her mind still was from the wine, she had a sense that only a Power greater than herself working through this particular state trooper could have gotten her the help she needed.

Rose never had another drink.

30
A Beneficial Mistake

IT WAS SHORTLY after Thanksgiving Day in 1975 when Angela, a thirty-seven-year-old computer programmer, began to sense that her whole life was slowly falling to pieces. And yet she continued to fight her addictions to alcohol and other drugs all by herself out of fear of losing her job, her son, and her self-respect should anyone discover her problem.

So, for the next six years, this single mom managed to drag herself to work every day and put on a good enough front to apparently fool most of the people in her office. Still there were many instances when she felt her office manager was watching her with deep suspicion while beginning to question the growing number of sick days she was piling up.

By the time the summer of 1981 rolled around, Angela's life was in shambles. Her feelings about herself and the life she was living were becoming too difficult to bear. Were it not for her twelve-year-old son, Jeremy, whom she deeply loved, she might have taken her own life.

It was in July when her manager took her aside and said she was concerned about Angela's health. She suggested Angela see a doctor. The manager also suggested that Angela take a three-week vacation to get away from the job pressure for a while. The manager said to choose the weeks that best suited her.

Despite her growing feelings of hopelessness, Angela also felt a deep longing to survive and get better. It started when one of the few close friends she had left planted the idea of going to an alcohol and drug rehab, something she had thought about herself from time to time. The three-week vacation period her manager suggested she take would be a perfect time to go, and no one would ever have to know about it.

She chose a period in late August, when her son would still be on his summer vacation from school, and made arrangements for him to stay with a friend. Then she found an excellent alcohol and drug rehabilitation hospital that could accept her at that time for its twenty-one-day program. In fact, it was the only opening they had for the next several months. She felt fortunate they could fit her in. It all seemed like it would work out perfectly.

As soon as she made the plans, Angela's mind filled with fear. How could she spend all that time away from a drink or a drug, she thought, when she hadn't spent a single day without something in her system for the last ten years? Would she be able to work or handle anything in life clean and sober? Perhaps her greatest fear was that she might fail at this attempt to change her destructive lifestyle and continue to drink and use forever.

The following weeks seemed to drag on and on. She thought many times about changing her mind about the rehab and simply going off to some resort with her son for a vacation. But something inside kept telling her she might not get another chance to get well and live a better life.

It was ten days before Angela was due to take off when her manager came into her cubicle with some upsetting news. She explained that something important had come up and she would have to leave town on business during the period Angela had chosen to "go on vacation." She was very apologetic but said that the programmer would have to change her plans since she wanted the entire staff in the office while she was gone. Her manager then suggested she take off the first three weeks of September.

When the manager left her cubicle, Angela's mind began racing. This could be her excuse for not going to the rehab. After all, it wasn't her fault she would have to cancel all the arrangements. And besides, her son would be back in school and who could care for him then? But that's when the guilt set in, the gnawing feeling that this could wash away any chance she might have of getting clean and sober. What should she do?

Angela couldn't sleep that night. She would have to call the rehab in the morning to cancel her arrangements and then try to find another facility that might be able to take her in September. Then she would have to find someone to care for her son while she was away and he was going to school. It all seemed so complicated that she had a few extra drinks to calm her nerves.

This desperate single mom didn't know at that time that God often does things for people that they cannot do for themselves. There was a phone message waiting for Angela when she arrived at the office the next morning. It was from the alcohol and drug rehab. When she called back, they told her they had made a mistake in the scheduling of incoming patients, that there was actually no room for her in August. They apologized and wanted to know if she could possibly come the first three weeks of September instead.

For a moment, Angela was speechless. The feelings that washed over her at that moment were almost impossible to describe, for she knew something very special had happened. Only later would she realize it was her Higher Power taking care of her. After she said yes to the rehab, she called a friend who said she would be happy to watch over her son while she was away.

That was fifteen years ago. Through the programs of Alcoholics Anonymous and Narcotics Anonymous, Angela hasn't had a drink or other drug since she left rehab. Her son is now twenty-seven and is married with two children. Angela also remarried and has a fourteen-year-old daughter. She still loves to tell the story of the "beneficial mistake" the rehab made, one that turned out to be a quiet miracle that changed her entire life.

31
Directions from Her Dearest Friend

JUDY AND LINDA were more than just first cousins. They were very best friends. They grew up together, and even when Judy moved away with her family, they would call, write, and visit as much as they could.

They drew even closer after both married. Whatever problems they had, they shared them with each other. Wherever one wanted to go, the other always seemed to tag along. They even shared their marital difficulties, not always agreeing on what should be done, but always supporting each other's decisions.

The thing that Judy and Linda did together most often was laugh. They found laughter in everything. Even during those times when things would get difficult and painful and there seemed to be no way out, they would look at each other and say, "This has gotten so ridiculous it's almost laughable." Then they would laugh—and they would feel better.

Linda's husband, Bruce, had heart disease as a young man, and it got worse as he grew older. They had two daughters, and after a while he could no longer play with them, take them to the park, or go on long trips. He became home-bound, tied to an oxygen tank. So Judy would take the girls shopping, to the movies, and generally help out while Linda stayed home taking care of her husband. Then the inevitable happened. Bruce had a massive heart attack and passed away. He was only forty-four. Linda was forty.

The funeral was a sad and painful experience. But Linda got through it with Judy at her side, surrounded by their loving families. After that, the days seemed to drag on and on. Judy was constantly searching for ways to make her best friend feel better, to find some cheer, some laughter. But it took awhile.

Since Linda's girls were now in high school, she decided to get a job to keep herself busy. Some men at her office would ask her out, but it was almost a year before she accepted and began to date again. It wasn't easy. As she told Judy, good, decent men seemed hard to find. It wasn't that she was that choosy. In fact, Judy was even choosier. She would nitpick practically every guy her friend dated.

And then Chuck came along. He was a retired police officer with two teenage boys, an ex-wife, and a red Mustang convertible. He was tall, heavyset, and somewhat good-looking. Linda was infatuated by his lavish attention, his sense of humor, and his free and easy lifestyle. But Judy didn't like him at all.

Right from the start, Linda's best friend thought Chuck drank way too much, talked constantly about his gun collection, which she found scary, and was constantly critical of his ex-wife, who had sole custody of their children. She also felt he was too possessive of Linda, calling her every day and wanting to know who else she was dating. But Linda remained taken by Chuck's amorous ways and wouldn't heed the warning signals Judy was sending her.

In fact, Linda got angry and had a brief falling out with Judy when she learned her friend had asked Linda's brother Richard, also a police officer, to see what others on the police force knew and thought about Chuck. Richard found out his sister's boyfriend had a bad temper, continued to carry a gun, and had an order of protection out against him, courtesy of his ex-wife. That's when Linda understood Judy's concerns and decided to cool things down a bit with Chuck.

The ex-cop, on the other hand, wanted to warm things up even more. When Linda backed off and suggested they stop dating for a while, Chuck would sit in his car parked in front of her house to see if she was going out with anyone else. When Judy learned he was stalking her friend, she urged Linda to get an order of protection against him immediately. Linda hesitated, not wanting to upset Chuck more than he already was.

After Linda worked late one evening, one of the young men in her office offered to drive her home. She accepted, only to learn the next day that after she had gone into her house, Chuck accosted the young man. He shoved him against a tree, showed him his police badge, and warned him that if he ever saw Linda again he'd be in serious trouble. That's when she finally got an order of protection against him.

It was two o'clock on a Friday afternoon when Chuck showed up at Linda's office. Everyone could tell he had been drinking. He begged her once again to drop the order of protection and go out with him. She refused and demanded that he leave the office or she would call the cops immediately. He pulled out his gun and shot her through the heart. As she lay dying on the floor, he shot her twice more in the head. Then, as the office staff dove behind their desks screaming out in fear and horror, Chuck put the gun into his own mouth and killed himself.

Judy fainted in her husband's arms when she heard the news. When she came to, she cried hysterically for hours on end until her husband, Tom, finally had to call the doctor and get some medication to calm her and help her sleep. She was numb throughout Linda's wake and funeral and the family gathering afterward. Every time she would try to speak, only painful, tearful murmurs came out. Even wrapped in her husband's loving arms, she felt lost and alone. It only got worse as the days, weeks, and months passed by. It was as though she had been robbed of the most precious thing in her life.

While Judy questioned God's decision to take her very best friend, her deep faith gradually led her to believe that Linda's spirit was somehow still with her. Every time she heard people laugh, she thought she heard Linda's laughter among them. Every time she saw a brilliant sunset—something Linda loved to watch—she thought of her best friend. But Judy wanted so much to feel her spirit, to know without a doubt that Linda was truly in God's hands.

Tom felt his wife needed to get away, to take a long vacation. He finally convinced her to visit with his family in Greece. It had been some time since they had been to the beautiful island of Crete where the family lived. She finally agreed, and when packing, she put a framed picture of Linda into her suitcase.

The day they were leaving, Tom had forgotten to fill up the gas tank. So on the way to the airport, they almost ran out of gas. He had to pull off the main highway and stop at a service station in a neighborhood that was totally unfamiliar to him. After filling his tank, Tom tried to find his way back to the main highway but got completely lost. They now feared they might arrive late at the airport and not be able to make their flight.

As they turned another corner, Judy spotted a police car parked across the way. She told her husband to pull up next to it and she would ask for directions. When she got out and walked toward the police car, the police officer inside also got out. Judy was stunned. It was Richard, Linda's brother. She burst out crying. Richard was also shocked to see Judy. He took her into his arms. After a moment he looked at her and smiled, "What are you doing in this neighborhood? Is everything all right?"

Judy wiped her eyes and smiled back. "Tom and I are on our way to the airport and we got lost. But I know everything's going to be okay now."

That's when they looked into each other's eyes and said almost simultaneously, "It has to be Linda who did this."

Somehow they both knew that Richard's sister and Judy's very best friend had brought them together this day to let them know she was watching over them and would always be with them whenever they needed her help. It was at that moment that Judy knew for certain that Linda was in God's hands.

Richard got back into his police car and led them to the airport that day. As Judy stared up into the beautiful blue sky, she sensed she had experienced one of God's quiet, little miracles, one that helped her understand her very best friend would be with her the rest of her life.

32
A Path through the Autumn Leaves

BY THE TIME his law class had ended that morning, Wayne's hands were trembling, and his brow was filled with perspiration. He badly needed his morning "fix." At the same time, he knew that the next drink might be the one that finally got him kicked out of law school. He had been given his last warning in September, and now it was mid-October. The autumn leaves were falling and he could be falling next.

As the young student hurried from the building, he just happened to bump into Rabbi Levinson, the middle-aged chaplain for this upstate New York college and law school. Wayne had no idea why he suddenly grabbed the rabbi's arm that morning and pulled him aside except for the panic and confusion that filled his head. He knew he needed help, and perhaps he thought this kind man could help him.

"Rabbi," he mumbled, "I think I have a drinking problem, and I don't know what to do about it. Please don't tell anyone, because if they find out, I could be kicked out of college. What should I do?"

Wayne was slightly taken aback by the rabbi's quick response: "Are you ready to do something about it right now, son?"

He surprised himself even more when he immediately replied without equivocation, "Yes, I am ready. I have to do something."

Before this moment in the young law student's life, he might have talked about the "possibility" of having a drinking problem. Or he might have naively said he was "studying the likelihood" that alcohol was playing too big a part in his life. He might have even considered—depending upon how many drinks he had—appointing a panel to study and advise him about his drinking habits. But to immediately admit he was ready to do something about his drinking shocked him as soon as the words left his lips. It was certainly a sign of his growing desperation.

Rabbi Levinson then suggested Wayne attend a meeting of Alcoholics Anonymous that evening and told him exactly where it was and how to get there. While he felt a little calmer at this point, the law student was a bit confused by the rabbi's final remark as he walked away. "I'll see you later," the rabbi said.

Sure enough, the first person Wayne spotted when he arrived at the off-campus AA meeting that night was the rabbi. Suddenly he felt less nervous and less like a low bottom crawler, although he was still a bit confused—that is, until he learned the campus chaplain had been a member of AA for many years and had helped many students like himself find sobriety and a new way of life. Then Wayne met a number of other young people at the meeting, which gave him additional comfort, hope, and encouragement.

Before leaving, Rabbi Levinson handed Wayne a small booklet that contained a listing of all the AA meetings in the area. The chaplain then offered him three suggestions: first, that he attend another meeting the next night; second, that he get down on his knees when he returned to his room and thank God for keeping him sober that day; and third, that he ask God in the morning to help him stay sober for another day.

That next morning, Wayne awoke shakier than ever and with an even stronger urge for a drink. *How am I going to get through my classes today like this?* his alcoholic mind kept asking him. *What am I going to do?* Then he remembered the rabbi's suggestions. He got down on his knees and asked God to help him stay away from drinking that day and make it to an AA meeting that night.

His last class ended at 3:00 p.m. He had gotten through so far, but now that urge was returning. He was determined not to drink, yet he felt like he was losing control. He realized that if he didn't get together with some AA people as soon as possible, he might drink. So he stopped at the campus library to use the phone. He called the chaplain's office and his room, but there was no answer. That's when the real panic began to set in.

Wayne rushed back to his own room to get the meeting booklet the rabbi had given him the night before. He would drive straight to an AA meeting. But he couldn't find the booklet. He practically ransacked the entire place searching for it, but it was nowhere to be found. Then he thought that maybe he left it in his car. So he ran into the parking area off the campus quadrangle and frantically scoured the interior of his car, including the glove compartment, between the seats, and under the seats. No AA meeting list.

As he stepped from his car, he felt the cold, misty air add to the shakiness he was feeling inside. The ground around him was covered with thick piles of wet leaves that had lost their brilliant autumn colors. The panic was getting worse. He remembered looking up into the heavy gray sky and murmuring, "Please, God, help me."

Then he took a deep breath and began walking slowly back toward his room, kicking despondently at the wet leaves under his feet. Suddenly, through his tearful and rather befogged eyes, he caught sight of something sticking out from under a pile of leaves. It wasn't the color of money, so whatever possessed him to bend down and pick it up he didn't understand at that moment. It turned out to be the AA meeting list he must have dropped the night before.

As he stood there looking at the soggy but still readable booklet, he now realized why he had picked it up. For finding it was no mere coincidence. He had asked for God's help, and he knew without a doubt that God had led him to it. He found himself at an AA meeting in a nearby church basement fifteen minutes later. He was early, but there were AA members there to talk with. He continued making meetings. After three months, the strong cravings to drink left him as he continued to be a very active member in the program of AA. He graduated from law school with honors.

Today Wayne is a very successful attorney. He believes more than ever after many years of sobriety that he experienced one of God's quiet, little miracles—one that helped him find a pathway to a sober life through those wet autumn leaves.

33
God and Santa Worked It Out

IT WAS THE first sober Christmas Vivian had celebrated in more than ten years. What made it even more special was finding a letter her twelve-year-old daughter Katie had written to "Santa Claus" and intentionally left under the Christmas tree for her mother to find.

The letter read: "Dear Santa. Thank you for all my Christmas presents, but thank you especially for the greatest present you could have possibly given me—a sober mother. Last year was the worst Christmas I ever had when my mother got drunk and fell into the tree. This Christmas is the best one I've ever had. Thank you, Santa. Katie."

Vivian kissed and hugged her daughter as tears of joy ran down her face. She had been sober now almost four months after making that last painful trip to another alcohol rehabilitation clinic. Now she was in the fellowship of Alcoholics Anonymous, making meetings and staying close to her sponsor.

Her husband, Ken, was almost as happy as their daughter. He still loved his wife very much and was relieved she had finally stopped drinking. But even after all these years, he never really accepted his wife's alcoholism as a disease. He still thought it was a matter of willpower and choice, perhaps because he was a rather heavy drinker himself who seemed able to control it—keep his job, meet his responsibilities, and not get too drunk at the wrong times like his wife always did.

Vivian and Ken held hands and laughed that morning watching Katie tear open one present after another. The spirit of Christmas filled the room. Vivian surprised her husband, an avid golfer, with a brand-new Big Ben driver, something he had been hinting about for months. Then it was his turn, a surprise for the whole family he thought would fill them with glee.

Ken announced he was taking his wife and daughter on a lavish Caribbean cruise over the New Year's holiday. He had been arranging it ever since Vivian left rehab. Katie jumped for joy, but Ken was a bit disappointed in Vivian's reaction. She forced a smile but didn't seem elated. Actually, she was suddenly filled with trepidation. When her husband asked why she didn't seem happy about his generous Christmas gift, Vivian claimed she was afraid of getting seasick. He assured her a few pills would take care of that situation.

They were to embark December 28 and bring in the New Year aboard a huge luxury liner. Since there were so few days to make preparations and pack suitcases for herself and her daughter, Vivian had little time to think about anything else, including calling her AA sponsor. Every time she thought about all the drinking and revelry she heard took place on cruises, she tried to put it out of her mind. Still, she had difficulty sleeping and was totally fatigued by the time the day for their departure arrived.

The plane flight and bus trip to the seaport went without a hitch. Katie's infectious enthusiasm captured her mother's attention, while Ken's constant descriptions of the islands the ship would be visiting actually stirred some excitement, which showed in Vivian's more relaxed demeanor. Also, she was trying to practice what the AA program had taught her thus far—to take it one day at a time and trust God.

The deluxe suite Ken had reserved aboard the liner was absolutely beautiful. There was an outside balcony replete with lounge chairs that overlooked the sun-bathed ocean. Also, Ken had arranged for a large bouquet of flowers to be placed in the cabin for her and a basket filled with fruits and sweets for Katie. Smelling the roses as the cruise ship slowly left the pier and headed for the blue Caribbean Sea, Vivian began to believe that this could be a really wonderful trip.

It wasn't until the next afternoon that Vivian's trepidation returned. As they lounged in the sun around one of the ship's five pools, she noticed the waiters ferrying all sorts of alcoholic beverages to her fellow sun worshippers. It was the same at dinner and at the cabaret show after dinner. And her husband's drinking only added to her growing stress.

Fortunately she remembered to pack her AA Big Book along with some spiritual literature. After tucking Katie into bed, Vivian read herself to sleep while her husband gambled and drank the night away at the ship's casino.

But the stress grew worse, and the thought of drinking started on their second day out when the cruise ship docked at a port in the Bahamas. While Vivian tried to enjoy a tour of the island with her daughter, her husband kept downing rum punches wherever they went. He continued his heavy drinking at dinner that night as he exchanged some off-color jokes with the people seated at the table with them. His drinking so upset his wife at this point that she excused herself before the food arrived and went to their suite.

Vivian's abrupt departure embarrassed her rather tipsy husband. When he finally returned to their cabin with Katie, he and his wife began to argue. He said all he was doing was trying to have a good time and just because she couldn't drink anymore was no reason for her to try to stop him. Their daughter began to cry. Their yelling began to bring back painful memories. That's when Ken turned and stormed out, heading back to the gambling casino. Vivian held Katie in her arms, trying to apologize.

The next morning Ken made his own apologies. He said he didn't realize how much his drinking upset his wife and that he would cut back, especially in front of her. They all hugged and went off to breakfast. But while Vivian felt a little better, the insidious disease of alcoholism was now working on her big time. The thought of having just one small glass of wine at dinner was beginning to obsess her. She couldn't get it out of her mind.

By now they had become quite friendly with the six people they dined with each evening. So when they arrived for dinner that night, they were in for a surprise. Two of the couples had bottles of vintage wine delivered to the table as thank-you gifts from the tourist agencies that had handled their travel arrangements. The couples offered to share the wine with the entire table. As the waiter began filling their wineglasses, Ken suddenly reached out and in a very overprotective manner covered his wife's wineglass with his hand, saying, "None for my wife. She can't drink alcohol."

Vivian's face reddened, and her eyes filled with tears. Inside, feelings of shame, weakness, and anger rushed through her. She sensed everyone staring in her direction. She pushed her chair back from the table, got up, and rushed out of the dining room.

She didn't want to return to their suite. She didn't want to see her husband and daughter. She didn't want to see anyone. All she wanted to do was get a drink. She started wandering aimlessly around the ship arguing with herself, trying to fight off that familiar urge to find oblivion and to find it in alcohol, the only thing she knew that could erase all her shame and painful feelings.

She found herself on the upper deck, approaching a bar filled with happy, laughing people. That's the way she wanted to feel, the way she knew a few drinks once made her feel. So she walked to the end of the bar and waited for the bartender to approach.

When he did, she ordered a vodka and tonic. The bartender smiled and said, "You'll have to go to another bar for that, ma'am. Tonight all we're serving here is coffee and soft drinks. You see, all these people here are on what they call a cruise without booze. They're all members of AA. Almost two hundred of them."

As he walked away, Vivian sat there for a moment with her

mouth open. Then she began to cry—not the angry tears she had been holding back, but tears of true gratitude. She knew instantly that this was God doing something for her that she could not do for herself.

Just then two women approached and asked if there were any way they could help her. She told them what had happened and about her urge to drink. The women led her to a nearby table, and before long it was like she had known them all her life. They, too, were members of AA and fully understood the struggle she was in. But now they told her the struggle was over. She no longer had to handle things all by herself.

For Vivian, the rest of the cruise really was wonderful. She now had members of AA to visit with and meetings to attend. And she was still able to enjoy her time with her husband and daughter. It made all things better. God and Santa found a way to turn this Christmas present into a trip of joy and freedom through another quiet, little miracle.

34
A Leopard Killed His Faith

FOR MORE THAN twenty years, Frank had been a loyal and faithful Christian missionary priest in East Africa, until one fateful day when it all suddenly changed.

Perhaps "suddenly changed" is the wrong way to describe what really happened. Actually, the once highly motivated and dedicated pastor had been having "faith troubles" for several years as he watched the poverty that surrounded him grow worse, not better. He began to find it difficult to understand why a loving God couldn't find some way to help the native people out of their tragic plight.

Every Sunday he would stand in an old, dilapidated church and preach about God's love and caring. After a while, looking out at the frail bodies and sad eyes of his congregants, he began to feel like a hypocrite, like his words didn't really ring true. The more he prayed and read the Bible and his spiritual books, the more he felt like his faith was leaking away. And the more poverty and helplessness he witnessed, the more the leak became a hemorrhage.

One day while visiting an outlying village, he happened to

notice some young boys in the distance playing in a heavy thicket. It was a place where wild animals would often hide while awaiting their prey. Suddenly he heard loud, roaring sounds coming from the thicket, then fearful screams as he watched the boys scatter in panic. He turned to see some older men quickly pick up spears and rush toward the thicket.

Hesitating for a moment, the missionary priest then followed them. When he reached the area where he heard the roars, he was horrified by what he saw. There on the blood-covered ground lay a fourteen-year-old boy he knew from the village, torn to pieces by a leopard the men were now chasing out into the plains. *Why,* he asked himself as he stared at the ravaged torso, *would God let something like this happen to such an innocent boy who was already experiencing such a difficult life?*

The minister could find few words to comfort the boy's distraught parents. They wanted to understand something even he couldn't comprehend in his growing state of disbelief. That was the day Frank's faith left him. It was killed by a leopard that savagely took a young boy's life. He stopped believing in his church, in its teachings, and in God Himself. He soon left the church, left East Africa, and returned to the United States.

Frank then met a lovely woman and fell deeply in love. They married. She gave the ex-priest the first real happiness he'd had in many years. She also gave him a son and daughter over the next few years, and his joy knew no bounds. Perhaps that's why he didn't object when his wife, very religious herself, wanted the children baptized in her church and educated in a Christian school.

It didn't seem to matter one way or the other to this former missionary. Whatever his wife decided about her and the children's religion was okay with him. In fact, to prevent too many questions about his own beliefs, he would go to services with them and join his wife at meetings with the teachers at school. But he himself got nothing out of it. He felt spiritually dead inside.

But Frank's wife had a deep faith in God and in her religion, and he knew she prayed constantly that his faith would return some day. In fact, she would tell him in those quiet, unguarded moments spouses share that if he would only look a little harder at the innocent beauty of their children and at their own deep and true love, perhaps he might find God there and believe in Him once again.

At her urging, he started to read the New Testament and a few spiritual books that meant so much to him at one time in his life. He would watch his children at play, take long walks down by the river, and stare at the beauty of nature in all its fulfillment. But during those restless nights, memories of his missionary work would come back and haunt him. He would relive all that poverty and suffering in East Africa and see that poor young boy torn apart by the leopard. While he struggled to regain his faith, it seemed to be a losing battle.

Then came another fateful day in Frank's life. His own son, also now fourteen years old, was running late for his Babe Ruth League baseball practice at a ball field not far from their home. Not looking as he rushed across a busy thoroughfare, he was struck by an oncoming car. He was critically injured and rushed to the hospital by ambulance. Frank was at his office when his wife called him with the terrible news.

The teenage boy was in a coma in the intensive care unit when his father arrived at the hospital. The doctors told him and his wife that their son had a serious head injury as well as broken ribs, a broken arm, and internal injuries. They said if he made it through the night, there was a chance he might recover.

While Frank stood next to his son's bed with his jaws clenched and his eyes filled with anger, his wife visited the hospital chapel to pray for the boy's recovery. When she returned, she suggested her husband also visit the chapel. She said it might give him some relief from the terrible rage he was expressing against a God he claimed he didn't really believe in.

Without speaking, Frank turned and left the ICU. He began pacing the hallways as tears of anger and confusion ran down his face. He could hardly breathe, he was so filled with painful mixed emotions. He stopped pacing for a moment and thought to himself, *If all the churches, cathedrals, grottos, and chapels in this world are supposed to be God's homes on Earth, then maybe I should visit this hospital chapel and tell Him exactly what I think.*

A few minutes later, the former pastor found himself standing in a quiet room with stained-glass windows, wooden pews, and a small altar up front. He was ready to berate his Creator for all the terrible injustices he saw around him, for all the pain and poverty in the world, and for not putting an end to all the hatred, bitterness, and distrust that was continuing to tear nations and people apart. And as all his rage was ready to pour out, he wanted to shout most of all about how unfair and cruel it was to take the life of that boy in East Africa and now possibly the life of his own son.

But for some reason the words wouldn't come. Instead, Frank suddenly heard a soft, gentle voice inside his head. The voice whispered, "Don't walk away from me again, Frank. Stay with me this time and pray. Let me help you understand that I am not to blame for all that you accuse me of. I am not a vengeful God. I am truly a loving God, and I will show you by making your son well."

For a moment, the former missionary priest stood motionless. Then he dropped to his knees and wept. He reached out his arms and began to say the Lord's Prayer. As he did, he saw his son darting out into traffic from behind a parked car. Instantly he knew it wasn't God's fault the boy was seriously injured. Then he saw the boy in East Africa taunting the leopard with a long stick, showing off in front of his friends. Once again he realized it was not God's fault, either, that the snarling leopard killed the boy.

Before Frank left the chapel that evening, he understood as he had never understood before that his Creator gave everyone free will and He allows them to make their own decisions and their own mistakes. But even in their mistakes and misdeeds, Frank realized that God still loves His people. Why did the former priest now understand so clearly? He was suddenly feeling God's unconditional love in his soul and the peace that comes with that love. In that instant, his faith returned.

Frank and his wife spent the entire night and early morning hours at their son's bedside in the ICU. It was almost dawn when they saw his eyelids flicker, then open wide. The young boy came out of his coma. God had performed another quiet, little miracle. The young boy completely recovered. So did his father, whose faith had not only been restored but also grew stronger as each day passed.

35
A Long Overdue Confession

EVERY CATHOLIC PARISH has an altar server or two who is tempted to taste the holy wine the priest uses when saying Mass. Tim was no exception. Only it became more than a mere temptation for this rather mischievous lad of twelve. It became a habit that grew out of hand.

Each Sunday morning, Tim would seclude himself in a corner of the church sacristy while filling the wine cruet the priest would use for Mass. Then he would put the wine bottle to his lips and take a long gulp. Then he'd take a second and usually a third. One particular Sunday, when he was about to take a fourth gulp, the young assistant pastor who was saying Mass that morning walked in and caught Tim red-handed.

"Now I know why the altar wine has been disappearing so quickly," the priest said rather sternly. Then he threatened to tell the boy's parents and drop him from the altar server society. Actually, the young priest was only trying to put the fear of God into the boy, whom he knew to be a school cutup and troublemaker.

While Tim pleaded for forgiveness, fear and anger were building up inside him. He hated to get caught. And he knew how much trouble he'd be in at home if the priest really told his parents what he had done. They were fairly lenient most of the time, but not when it came to anything having to do with church or God. Even though the priest said he would think it over, Tim felt he couldn't take any chances.

All that day his young but very fertile brain tried to figure a way out of this troublesome situation. One of the ploys he believed in—something he had gotten from his sports-minded friends—was that the best defense was a great offense. By that evening, he had it all plotted out. He started walking around the house with a deep frown on his forehead and a painful look on his face. He knew his parents would soon be asking what was bothering him, for he had manipulated them many times in the past.

When they finally did ask, Tim told them a calculated, bold-faced lie without ever considering what the consequences might be for himself or others. It was a lie woven out of the priest sex-abuse scandals he had seen on television and heard his parents talking about recently.

Tim told his mother and father that the assistant pastor had been hitting on him—making sexual advances and suggesting that they commit some bad and sordid acts. When he refused, he said the priest got very angry and started accusing him of doing things he didn't do, like stealing and drinking the altar wine. Tim said his friend Ricky knew all about it and would confirm his story.

Ricky was a timid and passive child whom Tim could easily

talk into vouching for his every word. Besides, he was a co-hort in stealing the altar wine and was fearful of what might happen if they ever got caught. Ricky was promised his secret would be kept if he went along with the story.

The very next day Tim's parents went to the church rectory and told the pastor they intended to press charges against his assistant. The pastor calmed them down and promised to investigate the matter immediately. Within days the situation was brought before the local bishop. Despite the young priest's protestations, the bishop took the charges very seriously, since the Catholic church's sex-abuse scandal was still very much in the public eye and also because there was an alleged witness to Tim's accusations.

It was decided after long and tortuous discussions that since there were no charges of actual physical abuse, the assistant pastor be relieved of his duties at the parish and be sent off to a monastery. There he would have no contact with young children. The parents agreed, and the matter was dropped.

But the episode left severe scars on everyone involved— not only the innocent young priest who loved his parish work, but especially on Tim. As the years went by, the former altar server felt more and more guilt as he came to realize the immense impact his lie had on so many lives. And the ruined and tainted life of the priest he falsely accused was always on his mind.

To handle his guilt and the other problems his mischievous and now out-of-control life caused him, Tim began drinking more and more as he grew from a teenager into an adult. He stopped going to church and soon lost all contact with God in his life. He found it difficult keeping trusting relationships with people, holding on to jobs, and living comfortably with himself without drinking.

By the time he was in his thirties, Tim was a full-fledged alcoholic who was getting sicker and sicker physically, mentally, and spiritually. He began making geographical changes, but no matter where he went, he couldn't get away from himself and the ghosts of the past that haunted him.

Having nowhere else to run and finally recognizing that drinking was his problem, Tim started coming to Alcoholics Anonymous meetings. After several attempts, he began to put some sober days together. He got a sponsor, found God again, and became serious about working the program's Twelve Steps of recovery in his life. When it was time to do his Fifth Step—"Admitted to God, to ourselves, and to another human being the exact nature of our wrongs"—Tim broke down and told his sponsor all about the false accusations he had made against a priest more than twenty years before.

His sponsor said he should try to find the priest and make amends in any way he could in order to cleanse his guilt and lead a sober life. Tim was living now in a different state. He started his search by first calling his family and past acquaintances, but no one knew where the priest had gone. The elderly pastor had long since passed away, and the bishop's office had no location for the former assistant pastor, since he had been sent out of state to a monastery. Tim even called the monastery, but the director said he didn't even know if the man was still a priest.

Even though Tim was only in his late thirties, the disease of alcoholism had taken a serious toll on him physically. He had a mild heart attack and now was suffering from painful angina. As the chest pains grew worse, his doctor put him into the hospital for more tests. The results showed he needed heart-bypass surgery right away.

The day before the operation, Tim decided he wanted to go to confession. Much of his past guilt was still with him, and he thought that confessing his sins to a Catholic priest—especially since the surgery was precarious and he might die—would lessen his guilt and give him some peace. So he asked to see the hospital chaplain.

While more than twenty years had gone by, Tim recognized the man the moment he walked into his room. He broke down and wept, for he knew this was his Higher Power working in his life. Why else would his former assistant pastor be standing at his bedside smiling down at him?

It was a confession long overdue, but it was God giving Tim a chance to make it to the very man he had harmed. And as he received absolution for all his past sins, he could tell that this loving priest held no resentments against him. He had long since forgiven the destructive words and actions of a young and troubled altar server.

The heart-bypass surgery was a complete success. It not only removed Tim's heart problems, but it also seemed to remove all his guilt. Of course his reconciliation with his former assistant pastor also helped. They remained good friends from that day on.

36
Help Was Right around the Corner

IT HAD BEEN a painful, downhill slide for almost a year and a half. Now Adam lay in a motel room trying to drink himself to death. His wife had finally followed through on the threat she had been making for some time and divorced him. What was left to live for when you've lost the only person you've ever truly loved?

It was Sunday afternoon, August 17, 1996, in Castle Rock, Colorado, and the booze had stopped working. The thirty-eight-year-old computer analyst couldn't get drunk and he couldn't get sober. The many bottles of scotch he drank to soothe his deep emotional pain were killing him mentally and spiritually but not physically, as he wanted. He got to his feet and staggered into the bathroom.

When he stared into the bathroom mirror, he hardly recognized the man staring back at him. His eyes were bloodshot, his face under a five-day growth of beard was blotchy and swollen, and his lips were puffy and cracked. His hands shook as he tried throwing cold water on his face and head. Adam had run out of scotch a few hours ago, and now it was decision time once again. Should he call the young clerk at the front desk and have him buy a few more bottles of scotch, or should he do what that inner voice had been telling him each time he awoke—to go back to Alcoholics Anonymous?

He dried his face and hair. Then glancing one more time into the mirror, he realized he couldn't go on like this. If he wasn't going to die, then he had better learn how to live. So he picked up the phone and called the front desk. This time, however, he even surprised himself. He asked the young man to get him some orange juice and hot chicken soup. He hung up, went back into the bathroom, and took the first shower he had in almost a week.

When he walked unsteadily into an AA meeting that night, an older man named Jimmy came over and shook his hand. He remembered Adam from the few meetings he had been to a year and a half before and welcomed him back. Jimmy was Italian with a thick Massachusetts accent. He had curly salt-and-pepper hair and dressed very sharply. Adam didn't remember him but was impressed by the older man's warmth and friendliness and the fact that he told it like it was.

They talked for quite a while after the meeting ended. Then Jimmy gave his younger friend his telephone number and told him to call if he ever needed a ride or needed to talk. Adam had no idea where the man lived but had a feeling of comfort and safety just having his phone number.

While Adam was now staying at a motel, he still had the house where he and his wife lived but had to sell it as part of the divorce settlement. So, after a few days of sobriety, he thought he had enough courage to go there and look around. He needed to decide what to keep, what to sell, and what to give away. He saw that his wife had already taken all of her personal things, so it was just a matter of some furniture, a few appliances, and his own clothes and personal items.

Rummaging through the kitchen, he happened to find some telephone bills in a cabinet drawer. He noticed there was an unfamiliar phone number on one of the bills that had been called quite a few times. Curious, he dialed the phone company's business office and learned the person's full name and address. Hesitating, he finally decided to call. A man's voice answered. Adam claimed he dialed the wrong number and hung up. He was devastated.

As he sank into a kitchen chair, he glanced at some of the other bills and found the same phone number on those also. That's when he realized how frequently his wife had been calling this other man—and probably seeing him on those weekends when she claimed she had been out shopping all day and sometimes late into the evening. He also recalled her "girls night out" every week when she said she was staying with various girlfriends. He was always too drunk to question or check her claims, but now it was apparent she had been cheating on him.

Adam broke down and started to cry. Then the tears turned from self-pity to anger and soon into rage. He began throwing things around the kitchen. His mind was becoming filled with crazy thoughts. He'd get the gun from his closet and blow his brains out. The gun wasn't there. He remembered that his wife had sold it. So he'd get some booze and pills instead and die from an overdose. There wasn't a drop of alcohol or a single pill in the whole house.

That's when Adam fell to his knees and asked for God's help. "Please God," he begged. "Please save me from myself."

For some reason he suddenly thought about Jimmy, the man he had met a few nights before at the AA meeting. Fighting the urge to flee from the house and into the nearest bar, Adam searched his wallet and found the older man's phone number. He called. Jimmy answered almost immediately. Adam felt relief come over him, the same feeling of comfort and safety he felt the night he met Jimmy.

Jimmy could tell Adam was upset and asked if he had had anything to drink. Adam said no, but that he couldn't get rid of his urge. He went on to explain finding the phone bills and how calling the man who had been seeing his ex-wife drove him crazy. When he talked about wanting to kill himself, Jimmy realized how much trouble his friend was in. He said his car was in the shop for repairs but that he would call a taxi and be right over.

When Adam asked where he lived, he couldn't believe the answer.

"That's right around the corner," he stuttered.

"Then give me your address, and I'll be there in a few minutes," his AA friend replied.

When Adam hung up, he knew that something special had just happened. Even though he wasn't a religious man and strayed far from a God he still believed in, he knew it was his Higher Power managing to get him help right away—and from a man he had probably seen in his neighborhood many times before but had never gotten to know until he needed him.

Jimmy was at Adam's house in less than five minutes. They talked for hours and then went to an AA meeting together. Adam still believes that God saved his life that day by sending him a man from around the corner who became his AA sponsor and his lifelong friend.

37
His Father's Secret

HIS DOCTOR DIAGNOSED it as a mild heart attack but also as a serious warning for a type A personality. In fact, he told Harold that he either learn to relax and enjoy life or the strain and tension he was bringing on himself from constant worry would result one day in a fatal massive thrombosis.

That ominous prediction made Harold worry even more.

Almost everyone who knew this pleasant and kind forty-eight-year-old businessman from Raleigh, North Carolina, would tell you he had every reason to be relaxed and happy, even joyful, about his life and all that God had given him. He was married to his beautiful high school sweetheart, had two gorgeous teenage daughters, and had a good-looking, athletic son who would soon be going off to college on a football scholarship.

He also had a successful wholesale furniture business and a large, comfortable home in the nearby countryside. Yet, for some unexplainable reason, Harold couldn't stop worrying about almost everything in his life. He had always been somewhat of a perfectionist, concerned about proper diet, proper exercise, proper health habits, proper dress, and proper life-style. But gradually, these "proper concerns" started turning into obsessive worries.

When their first baby daughter came down with a bad cold, Harold was sure it was pneumonia and rushed her to the hospital emergency room against his wife's better judgment. It was only a cold. When his son fractured his arm in a high school football game, he wanted him to quit the team and take up golf because it was a safer sport.

When the worried businessman got his first bleeding stomach ulcer, he was convinced it was cancer. It wasn't. And when his wife had a small fender bender while driving home from shopping one evening, Harold suggested she have her eyes checked to make sure she could see well driving at night.

He often worked late hours at his factory and sometimes even on weekends. His wife was constantly urging him to take a real vacation—a few weeks, not just a few days. He was insistent, however, that he needed to keep an eye on things. The truth was he had an excellent management team that also thought he needed time off, but no one could persuade him—that is, until he had his heart attack.

His family doctor, who had been prescribing mild sedatives for his nerves, suggested he take his wife on a ten-day cruise, away from telephones, faxes, and any other sort of contact with his furniture factory. His wife also thought it would be a wonderful way for both of them to relax and for her husband to recover. But Harold insisted he couldn't take that much time off. He did agree, however, to their spending a week at a Miami Beach resort. The problem was, he called his office every day and sometimes twice a day.

Then came the catastrophe of September 11, 2001, when terrorists crashed planes into New York's Twin Towers, not only taking down both skyscrapers and killing thousands of innocent people, but also taking the entire country down as well. The stock market crumbled, the nation fell into a deep recession, and Harold wound up in the hospital once again with severe chest pains. He feared that everything he had worked for would soon be in ruins and he and his family left destitute.

While it wasn't another heart attack, Harold's physician put him on a heavier dose of Valium and urged him to see a psychiatrist. The doctor thought Harold needed more than medical help to find a solution to his fears of impending doom. Harold agreed and saw a psychiatrist for several months, but it didn't help.

One of his very best friends, a deeply religious man, tried to drag him back to the church Harold had left some years before, telling him that God and prayer would soothe his soul. Harold insisted God caused most of his problems in the first place, which was why he didn't attend church. It seemed everyone wanted to help this confused and bewildered man, but no one had the answer, especially his wife. Now she was worrying too, mainly about her husband and the obsession that was gradually killing him.

Then came the news of Harold's father. While he lived in

Michigan, they were close and went fishing together every summer and fall. His father had contracted a radical form of leukemia but insisted that no one in the family tell his son about it because "He'll only fret over something he can't do anything about. I'll tell him myself when I get well."

But his father didn't get well. He quickly took a turn for the worse. That's when Harold's two older sisters finally called and suggested he come to Michigan as soon as possible. The doctor thought it might be only a matter of a few weeks or less before their father passed away.

Harold was very angry at first that he hadn't been told sooner about his father's illness. His sisters fibbed a bit, saying it all came on rather suddenly and that at the age of seventy-nine, their father had little strength to fight it.

By the time Harold and his wife arrived from North Carolina, his father, who was in hospice care at home, had already slipped into a coma. He and his sisters decided to take turns sitting by his bedside, watching and waiting. He vividly recalls that Wednesday morning. It was almost 3:00 a.m. He was half dozing when he noticed his father slowly opening his eyes and turning his face toward him. He was stunned because the doctor had told the family only that afternoon that their father would most likely not come out of his coma but would quietly pass away in his sleep.

"Dad!" he remembered saying as tears ran down his cheeks. "It's Harold. Can I get you something?"

That's when his father reached for Harold's hand to pull him close.

"Harold," his father whispered. "I'm glad you're here. I have something I must tell you."

His son waited while his father licked his dry lips with his tongue so that he could speak understandably. Then he tugged again on his son's hand to pull him even closer.

"You worry too much," he said. "You always have. I want to tell you my secret. I discovered a long time ago that most of the things I worried about never ever happened. I found out that worrying is a whole lot of wasted time and it's bad for you. So I stopped worrying. I turned all my cares over to God and had a real happy life. I want you to do the same. Promise me you will, because if you don't, you'll be dead before I am."

Harold squeezed his father's hand and replied in a choked voice, "I will, Father. I promise."

As he uttered those words, he recalls seeing a slight smile at the corner of his father's mouth. Then the elderly man closed his eyes and slipped back into his coma. He died a few hours later, surrounded by his family.

Harold knew before his father left him that something very special had happened early that Wednesday morning when he woke for those brief moments and spoke with him. During the funeral services at church, he came to realize it was God trying to free him from worry through his dying father's words. Flying back home to North Carolina that weekend, as he stared out the window into a beautiful cloudless sky, he knew he had experienced a miracle that was already starting to change his life.

From that day on, Harold worried less and prayed more.

He no longer feared what he might lose but became increasingly grateful for all that God had given him and his family. He regained his health and his faith and the kind of happy, peaceful life he thought he would never have. And it was all because he learned his father's secret through another of God's quiet, little miracles.

38
Has Anybody Got a Dime?

THINGS HADN'T BEEN going well for Charlie on two fronts—at home and on the job. He was a traveling salesman who was barely hanging on to his once lucrative territory in south Florida. His heavy drinking had put a serious dent into his sales calls and also caused too many missed meetings with important customers. At this point, his company was giving him one last chance to clean up his act and rebuild his sales volume.

At the same time, Charlie's wife was sick and tired of his never being home. She was used to his business travel schedule, but now, with his drinking often out of control, he wasn't even part of the family on weekends. All the chores and responsibilities—taking care of the house, their four children, the shopping—fell on her shoulders twenty-four hours a day, seven days a week. She was getting very bitter.

In addition to all this, his sales were dropping, the paychecks were getting thinner and thinner, and the debts were piling up. His wife sensed the major problem was all the money her husband was spending on alcohol, at home and on the road. She was at her wit's end.

Under growing pressure on both fronts, Charlie was doing everything he could to find new customers. There was one large company not far from his home that he had been calling on for months without making any progress at all. Then one day he heard that the sales manager, whom he didn't get along with, was fired and a new one was just hired. He stopped by and made an appointment to have lunch with the new manager.

As was his habit, Charlie arrived at the restaurant early to have a martini or two to ease the shakes. He was in quite a mellow mood when his potential new customer arrived. His name was Reid. The traveling salesman asked what he'd like to drink and was surprised when Reid asked for iced tea. As their conversation progressed, it turned out the new sales manager didn't drink alcohol. When pressed by his inquisitive luncheon companion, Reid replied rather unabashedly that he once had a serious drinking problem and was now a member of Alcoholics Anonymous. He was also quietly "carrying the message" to the man across the table whose hands, he noticed, wouldn't stop trembling.

Charlie was dumbfounded by the reply and almost knocked over his third martini. He didn't know what to say. He knew about AA and even thought about going to a meeting some months back after another terrible argument at home. But the next day, when things calmed down and he was feeling a little better, he just continued with his pattern of denying he really needed help—telling himself that he could control his drinking problem on his own.

But now, staring across the table at this healthy, happy-looking, and obviously very successful sales executive who was about his own age and was openly admitting he was an alcoholic, Charlie and his denial were being tested. He suddenly sat erect in his chair and replied with absolute honesty, "Reid, I can't stop drinking, and I don't know what to do about it."

"Do what I did," his newfound friend said. "Admit you're licked and join us. I promise you, Charlie, AA can get you sober and keep you sober."

Not only did the traveling salesman find an important new customer that day, but he also found the man who became his AA sponsor from the first meeting he attended—which was that very night.

They discovered they lived only ten miles apart, so they had no problem making meetings together or gathering at their respective homes to study AA's Big Book or work on the program's Twelve Steps of recovery. They always kept their business discussions separate from their talks about sobriety.

Since Charlie had to continue his extensive travels to serve what was now a growing roster of customers, Reid put great emphasis on them staying in touch by phone. He insisted his sponsee call him at least several times a week from wherever he was and more frequently if he was having any problems or got an urge to drink.

Things had gotten a little better at home now that the paychecks were getting larger and Charlie was returning home earlier from his sales trips, since he was no longer stopping to spend time in bars. But his wife still couldn't understand why he had to attend AA meetings on weekend nights. Before AA, he was spending weekends drunk on the couch. Now he was spending them at meetings. She grew resentful that he still had so little time for her, and she let him know it.

One day Charlie suggested to his wife that she go to Al-Anon, a program that helps families of alcoholics recover from the disease of alcoholism. She threw a pot at him, shouting that she didn't need any help. All she needed was a husband. The arguments continued. The only time Charlie seemed to find any peace was when he was on the road or at a meeting with his sponsor.

He soon found himself calling Reid almost every day, especially when on sales trips or after sessions with difficult customers. They would often talk about Charlie's wife and what he could do, if anything. Reid had no real answers for him except that he should say the Serenity Prayer more often. Still, the salesman found some solace in their talks.

One evening, while traveling between towns, he stopped for dinner at a small café near the Florida Everglades. After eating, he phoned his wife to say he'd be home a day earlier than he expected and perhaps they could do something special. He thought the news would make her happy. Instead, his wife complained about never knowing his schedule anymore, when he'd be home or not be home, when he'd be at his "damn" meetings or spending time with his sponsor. She went on and on until it became a screaming argument over the telephone.

Charlie finally slammed down the phone. His hands were shaking and his heart was pounding in his chest. He needed some fresh air. After walking in circles outside the café for a few minutes, he calmed down. So he got into his car and began driving toward the next town, which was past the end of the Everglades, about thirty miles away.

He hadn't driven more than five minutes when he felt the anger returning. That screaming argument with his wife had filled him with resentment, which was now turning into rage. He began pounding on the steering wheel. Then came the urge to drink. He glanced around, but there wasn't a bar in sight. He was in no-man's land. There was nothing but a swamp on both sides of the road. The next thought was to call his sponsor. He knew Reid could calm him down. He always did. But this was before cell phones, and he didn't know where could he find a phone out there.

The thought of calling his sponsor had no sooner entered his mind when up ahead in the darkness he spied a dim light off to the side of the road. As he drew close, he couldn't believe his eyes. There stood a telephone booth in a small safety area just off the shoulder. He jumped from his car, ran to the phone booth, and reached into his pocket for a dime—the cost of a phone call back then. He gulped when he saw that all he had were three pennies and a nickel. A deep depression came over him as he stared at the phone. He tried to say the Serenity Prayer, as Reid had often urged him to do on such occasions, but the words wouldn't seem to come.

After a moment, he started to walk away. Then, as so many people do almost automatically, he turned back and stuck his finger into the coin slot. He couldn't believe it. There was a dime in the slot. Instantly he knew his Higher Power was watching out for him. For Charlie that night, there was no other explanation.

Charlie was in for another wonderful surprise when he reached his sponsor a few moments later. It seems Charlie's wife called Reid after their terrible argument on the phone. She admitted she was so mean and nasty that she feared she might have driven her husband to take a drink. She asked his sponsor what she should do. He suggested she go to an Al-Anon meeting, and if it was okay, he would have a woman call her.

When Charlie arrived home sober two days later, his wife met him at the front door with warm hugs and tearful kisses. She told him she had attended her first Al-Anon meeting the night before, and though she cried a lot, she loved it. They forgave each other for all the mean things they had said and agreed to start another new day together.

Charlie believes today, without any doubt, that God had given him more than just a dime that night as he stood in that lonely phone booth in the middle of Florida's Everglades. He knows his Higher Power performed a quiet, little miracle that changed not only his life but also the lives of his entire family.

39
He Was Thrown a Curve Ball

IT'S EXTREMELY PAINFUL for a father to watch his teenage son suffer from a flagrant injustice, but it's particularly painful when the father is part of the problem. That was the situation George found himself in when his sixteen-year-old son, Marty, a fine baseball pitcher with great future prospects, was cut from the American Legion All-Star baseball team.

The situation made no sense at all to Marty or to any of his teammates since he had been the team's first-string pitcher all season. When the head coach refused to offer any explanation and all of Marty's pleas fell on deaf ears, the upset teenager turned to his father for help. The boy was devastated when he learned that his father played a major role in the problem.

George had been the assistant coach of his son's American Legion team. When it came time to select the all-star players for the upcoming state championship tournament, George began having run-ins with some of the parents who had boys on the team. It seemed almost everyone felt their sons should be selected. In some cases George didn't agree. In fact, he even thought the head coach's son didn't quite measure up and voted against him. That's when the political baseball wars really heated up and adults started acting worse than their children.

George, a former college all-star baseball player himself, knew the team would be facing serious competition in the state tournament, and therefore, only the very best players should be chosen. Even though everyone recognized that his son was by far the best pitcher, many still accused him of nepotism.

Backed by some disgruntled parents, the head coach asked George to resign as his assistant in order to create what he called "much-needed harmony." The real truth was he thought that between this request and cutting Marty from the team, it would put enough pressure on George to change his votes. But he didn't. George agreed to step down as assistant coach after making sure that according to the rules, the votes he cast would still count. Once again this made some parents very angry, but George didn't budge. He was a man of principle.

The most difficult part of the entire situation was trying to explain to his son why he didn't make the team when the young man had nothing to do with the squabble among so-called adults. When he asked Marty if he wished him to change his mind so he could get back on the team, the teenager simply shook his head no. He loved and respected his father, and despite his deep disappointment, he knew his father was right.

What made things even harder was the fact that the American Legion All-Star tournament drew a host of college baseball coaches and professional scouts looking for promising talent. Marty had been hoping to get a college baseball scholarship and now his hopes were dimmed.

In addition to being a man of principle, George was also a man of faith. He believed deeply that God would always make things turn out the way they were supposed to if you put the problem into His hands. While it was difficult convincing his son to let God handle things, they did agree to pray about it.

It was also difficult for George to watch his son try to ignore all the bitterness and angry talk going on among his friends and their families. The young pitcher began to isolate, staying in his room reading or on the computer. He also began to question whether or not he still wanted to play baseball anymore or perhaps put his focus and energy into another sport or activity.

About two weeks after Marty was cut and his team went on to lose in the first round of the all-star tournament, his father received a phone call from a good friend who was an alumnus of Old Dominion University. His friend had just received word that the school was hosting a pitchers and catchers camp. He knew everything that had happened and felt the camp might prove a pleasant distraction for Marty.

At first Marty said he didn't want to travel the several hundred miles to participate in a sport he was seriously thinking about giving up. His father knew that was only because his son was still suffering from all the hurt and disappointment. He told Marty the camp might help him decide one way or the other about playing baseball. He also said Old Dominion was a college he should check out.

George prayed even harder that night for God to remove all the hurt and injustice his own difficult decision had brought on his son. Over breakfast the next morning, the young pitcher told his father he would like to make the trip after all. It turned out to be an incredible weekend—one George was certain God had planned. It proved again to him and his son that when God closes one door, He surely opens another.

Much to their surprise, the event at Old Dominion University drew a large number of college coaches and major league scouts who were in the market for good pitching and catching prospects. Marty turned out to be one of them. Not only did the radar guns clock his throws among the highest of all the sixteen-year-old pitchers who were at the camp from all over the Atlantic Coast, but the young prospect was also given a great honor. He was asked by the scout for the Chicago White Sox at the camp's closing ceremonies to demonstrate his pitching delivery for the other young pitchers there.

The next day as they drove across the Chesapeake Bay Bridge on their way home, George's eyes filled with tears when his son turned to him and said, "Mr. Ford, the White Sox scout, said I'll probably be drafted into the major leagues right out of college. Wouldn't that be great, Dad? And I owe it all to you."

George said a silent prayer of thanks, not because of what might happen, but because of what already did happen. In just a few short weeks, this proud father and his talented son had traveled from the depths to the heights, and they both knew it was no mere coincidence. It was another one of God's quiet, little miracles.

Marty was offered a four-year baseball scholarship to Penn State University, which he accepted. In his senior year, he severely tore the rotator cuff in his pitching arm, ending his dreams of a major league career. Though deeply disappointed, he accepted it as God's will—that his Creator had something else in mind.

Marty graduated Penn State with honors and was a Rhodes Scholarship finalist. Today the once promising baseball pitcher works with Teach for America in a rural Louisiana high school. He's happy to be helping needy young people who are also thrown a curve ball in life. He and his father remain avid baseball fans.

40
The Wrong Six-Pack

It seemed like the longest twelve months of his life, going without a driver's license after being arrested and convicted of his second DUI (driving under the influence) offense. Now Mark finally had his license again and he was back in the driver's seat.

The problem was, however, that having his license renewed wasn't about to change most things in his life, including his attitude toward drinking alcohol. For a while he had been forced to attend "drunk driving classes" with others who had been charged with a DUI, but little sank in. He came away totally unconvinced that he had a serious drinking problem. He certainly wasn't an alcoholic. That's what those winos and derelicts were who hung out on street corners with a tin cup begging for handouts.

Mark told himself he still had a wife and family, a good job, some money in the bank, and a fairly new car. Okay, so the car had a few dents in it from skimming a telephone pole late one night and hitting his brick mailbox early one morning. But nothing really serious had happened—not yet anyway.

After his first DUI, he and his wife began arguing more and more about his missing dinner, coming home drunk, and waking up the children. Some Monday mornings she couldn't get him up for work because he drank too many beers on Sunday. Mark, in his denial, accepted the yelling and screaming as part of married life, and all his drunken buddies at the neighborhood bars agreed with him.

It had only gotten worse after he was arrested for his second DUI charge. His wife demanded he get help. She even suggested he call Alcoholics Anonymous and find out where they had meetings. He became infuriated at her inference that he was an alcoholic like those bums he always referred to whenever the subject of his drinking came up. He became even more infuriated when he learned his wife was going to Al-Anon, the program that helps spouses and families of alcoholics.

While he refused to admit it, deep inside Mark knew that getting his second DUI and losing his license for a year should have been a wake-up call. But even the embarrassment of attending those "drunk driving classes" and being forced to pee in a cup so those in charge could check if he had had a drink or a drug didn't shake his denial. He just couldn't face being an alcoholic, plain and simple.

When he first lost his license, it wasn't too difficult to stay away from the booze for a while. The threat of jail time and the desire to drive again were both strong incentives. Also, there had been a little more peace at home; he had dinner with his family every night, spent time with his children on weekends, and took his wife to dinner and a movie once in a while. But after a few months, when his classes ended, the urge to drink returned with a vengeance. It became "gritted-teeth sobriety."

Mark started counting the days on his office calendar when he would finally get his license back. Then he would no longer be under the spotlight, either at home or by the police. Then he might have a nip or two just to relax and have some inner peace. He didn't think that marking his calendar and obsessing for a drink might be signs of a serious problem with alcohol. And if the thought did occur, he quickly put it out of his mind.

Then came the day when he arrived home and found the letter from the Department of Motor Vehicles telling him his license had been reinstated. It was a reason to celebrate. By this time, however, his wife had gotten used to a sober husband and the children were enjoying a sober father—gritted-teeth or not. So when Mark suggested one Saturday night that a bottle of wine might go nice with dinner, his wife's face paled and his oldest daughter glared at him. While Mark didn't immediately express his angry feelings over their reaction, a deep resentment began to grow inside of him.

Resentments are like poison to an alcoholic. All that week the poison spread throughout Mark's system and deep into his alcoholic brain. By the following weekend, he was a walking time bomb. His wife lit the fuse that Friday night when she simply remarked how nice it was that he wasn't drinking anymore. Mark exploded, shouting that he wasn't an alcoholic, that he wasn't depriving his family of anything, that he could drink anytime he wanted to, and that if she didn't like it, it was just too damn bad!

With that, he stormed out of the house, jumped into his car, and took off. That night Mark actually drove past eight bars as he fought with the demons in his head. Since he had been going to church with his wife and family over the past few months, he thought about asking for God's help and direction. The trouble was, he already believed that God didn't want him to drink and the urge was now almost uncontrollable—especially with the resentment still eating away at him. He started to pray, but then he spotted one of his favorite drinking haunts just ahead.

He swung into a parking place near the bar and hurried in. There was something different about his old haunt that night. He noticed it was filled with women. There were no guys in sight. The bartender told him it was "Ladies Night" and that no men would be served until after 10:00 p.m. It was now only 6:00 p.m. The news threw more coals on Mark's burning resentment.

He left and got back into his car to find another bar. That's when he noticed a package store across the street with a neon sign that read "Harry's Place: Cold Beer and Soda." He figured a six-pack of beer would at least calm his nerves until he found another haunt. So he made a U-turn and pulled up in front of the store. His head was pounding and his face was filled with perspiration as he hurried inside.

He went to the large cooler in the back, grabbed a six-pack, and brought it to the counter. The young clerk looked at him and said, "That'll be one dollar and sixty-five cents."

"Wow!" Mark said, very surprised. "This beer is so cheap maybe I ought to get two six-packs."

"What beer?" the clerk frowned. "This is a six-pack of Coca-Cola."

Mark glanced down. Sure enough, he had grabbed a six-pack from the wrong cooler by mistake. Or was it a mistake? His eyes began to moisten. This was no coincidence. This was God doing for him what he couldn't do for himself, and Mark realized it almost instantly.

The man with two DUIs didn't drive right home that night. Instead, he looked up the phone number for Alcoholics Anonymous, found there was a meeting he could make that was close by, and went. That was more than twenty years ago.

Today Mark still drinks soda, still has his wife and family, and now has his own business. Much has changed for the better in his life because of God's quiet, little miracle in the package store that night when he picked up the wrong six-pack.

41
A Gift from a Wino

WES COULDN'T REMEMBER the last time he even thought about God or anything spiritual. His life was in shambles from his alcoholic drinking, and even those "foxhole prayers" he used to say out of sheer desperation had long since become like ashes on his tongue.

Twice divorced with two children who wanted no part of him, the fifty-five-year-old former army sergeant was having difficulty holding down a low-paying job at a neighborhood dry cleaners. Fortunately the owner was also a drunk. Wes was behind on his rent, had no real friends, and was rapidly getting sicker physically and mentally. He was already dead spiritually.

For the past six months he had been bouncing in and out of the fellowship of Alcoholics Anonymous. He freely admitted he was an alcoholic and had been for years, but his baffling and powerful disease kept telling him it was too late to change, that all was lost and could never be recovered. He would come to AA meetings for a week, then get drunk for a week. He would come late, sit in the back of the room, and leave early so he wouldn't have to say the Lord's Prayer at the end of the meeting. He no longer believed in all the God stuff, but he still enjoyed the coffee and cookies.

There was one particular guy named Artie, a tall, balding man about his own age, who would always grab him before the meeting and tell him how the Twelve Steps got him sober and how living the AA program changed his whole life. He seemed like a warm and sincere man, but he talked too much about a Higher Power for Wes's liking. One night he asked Wes for his phone number. Wes gave it to him reluctantly, telling himself he wouldn't answer anyway even if he called. Artie then stuck his own number into Wes's shirt pocket, telling him to phone before taking his next drink.

The following Saturday, just before Wes was about to embark on another weeklong binge, Artie did call. For some unexplainable reason, Wes picked up the phone. Artie said he needed some help. He was on his way to see a very sick and down-and-out wino. He asked Wes to come along in case there might be a problem. He also promised to buy Wes lunch before they got to the wino's place.

Since there wasn't much to eat in his shabby apartment and his television set was on the blink again, Wes agreed to go. At least those were the reasons he gave himself. As they sat in a local Greek diner eating lunch, Artie explained what a "Twelfth Step call" was—carrying the message of sobriety to another sick alcoholic. He said he expected the call on the wino would be a tough case. He wasn't kidding.

They found the poor, sick alcoholic in a basement hovel, lying in a dirty bed on filthy sheets, with big, oozing wine sores on many parts of his body. His hands and legs were trembling, and he smelled like week-old fish. Wes had never seen anything so disgusting. He began to regret volunteering for the assignment, especially when they carried him into a smelly bathroom and tried to clean him up as best they could.

Leaving the wino soaking in the tub, Artie opened the basement windows to air the place out and then started to clean it up. He asked Wes to take the dirty sheets, towels, socks, and underwear around the corner to a Laundromat they had spotted on their way. As he left the basement with a pile of stinking laundry, he couldn't believe he was doing all this. Then, though he didn't understand it at the time, he began to feel good inside for doing it.

After finishing the laundry, Wes returned to watch Artie treating the wino like his long-lost brother—drying him down, putting on clean underwear, and laying him back down under freshly washed sheets. Then he started talking to the half-out-of-it man about alcoholism, that it's a disease that kills people, that a loving God is giving him another chance at life, that AA can get him sober, and that he and Wes would show him the way if he was willing to try.

The wino refused to go to the hospital, so Artie and Wes stayed with him until late that evening, feeding him orange juice with Karo syrup and reading him passages from AA's Big Book. Then two of Artie's AA friends arrived to stay with the man through the night in case he went into the D.T.'s and they would have to get him medical assistance. Wes couldn't even explain to himself why he came back to the wino's place with Artie the next day. And he could hardly believe his eyes when they entered. In just twenty-four hours, the man was sitting up and drinking hot soup. He smiled warmly when he saw Artie and Wes walk in, which once again made Wes feel strangely good inside.

Over the next few weeks, as Wes kept coming back with Artie, who had now become his AA sponsor, he watched one of God's quiet, little miracles unfold. The wino's sores began to disappear, and the man got up and started going to AA meetings despite all his pain. Before the month was out he had put on some weight and was showing signs of becoming a healthy human being again. All the while, Artie kept saying it was just another case of God doing for someone what he couldn't do for himself.

As Wes watched and listened, he came to believe. He realized that there really was a loving God who not only helped the wino get well but healed Wes's soul at the same time. He also realized the wino had given him a wonderful gift: a restored faith.

By watching his Higher Power perform this quiet, little miracle with his very own eyes, Wes was able to break through his spiritual roadblock. He accepted the fact that he was totally powerless over alcohol and most other things in his life. And he made a decision to turn his will and his life over to the care of a God he had now come to know and love.

Wes and the wino stayed sober from that point on.

42
He Found Help at a Lunch Counter

A BUMP IN the road brought Joe out of a deep, groggy sleep. His neck was stiff from resting against the back of the car seat and his mouth had a foul taste in it.

He glanced over and saw his wife, Sandra, driving. Her jaws were clenched, and there was an angry look in her pretty blue eyes. Then he turned and looked out the car window at the beautiful Pennsylvania countryside. That's when it all came back to him. They were on their way home from a resort in the Pocono Mountains where they had gone to celebrate their first wedding anniversary. The weekend ended with a terrible argument over his heavy drinking.

Joe straightened himself up in his seat and lit a cigarette.

"Would you please put that out?" his wife said with anger resonating in her voice. "It bothers me when you smoke in the car."

He dashed the cigarette out in the ashtray and replied, "Would you like me to drive for a while?"

"No," she said. "I'm fine. You can just pass out again if you like."

With that sarcastic remark, Joe realized there was nothing more to say at the moment. He put his head back against the car seat and tried to reconstruct the past four days. It was now Sunday afternoon. They had come to the Poconos on Thursday to celebrate two things: their first year of wedded bliss and his recent graduation from law school, which had been a real struggle. He was a New York City cop before working his way through night school to get his law degree. He was already twenty-nine when he met and married Sandra, who was five years younger.

By then Joe was a rather heavy drinker. His new wife thought he was simply a guy who liked to celebrate life and that he'd ease off the sauce once he became a married man with responsibilities. That, by the way, became a third reason for them to celebrate in the Poconos—his latest responsibility. His wife broke the news at dinner Thursday night. She was expecting their first child. Joe didn't draw a sober breath for the rest of their trip.

The new lawyer wound up celebrating too much. He embarrassed his wife at dinner Saturday night by getting so drunk that he tried to dance with a cute waitress. Then he staggered up on stage and sang off-key with the country music band. Meanwhile, Sandra left the dining room and went to bed. When her husband finally got back to their room early Sunday morning, he threw up all over the bathroom floor. She had to clean it up.

Joe brought flowers home from work that Monday night. He also got down on his knees and begged Sandra to forgive him. He promised he would never have another drink. She cried in his arms and forgave him.

Soon, they had a son they named Daniel. The young lawyer kept his promise and stayed sober for the next two years. It wasn't easy, but the benefits of seeing his law practice grow, moving from a barely furnished garden apartment into a lovely new home, and the joy of watching his son take his first baby steps were compensations that made it all worthwhile.

However, when the pressure times came, like fighting a tough case in court or rushing Daniel to the hospital with a high fever, Joe had nothing to calm his nerves. And their nights out with friends weren't as much fun as they used to be. He had become what his wife called a "wet blanket," and he was prone to argue at the drop of a hat. He often felt like a martyr, sacrificing something he really enjoyed to please a wife who didn't show much appreciation. At least that's the way his cunning and creeping disease of alcoholism saw it.

Then came the Fourth of July. They were invited to a cookout at a friend's home across town. It was a very hot and humid day. His host handed Joe an icy cold bottle of beer. Without hesitation, the young lawyer put the bottle to his lips and downed half of it in one gulp. Sandra was shocked. She pulled him aside and asked why he was starting all over again when he promised he wouldn't. Somehow her husband convinced her that after two years of not drinking, he had everything together. Now he could handle one or two beers at a neighborly cookout without going overboard. After all, look at their life now. The least she could do was trust his judgment. Never again would there be a problem with booze.

For almost two months Joe controlled his drinking as he promised he would. But that Labor Day weekend at their in-laws, he had a few scotches with his father-in-law and it was off to the races. A few scotches became more than a few martinis and more than a few martinis became a few weekend drunks. The arguments started all over again, creating resentments that led to even more heavy drinking.

One Monday morning the lawyer awoke with the usual pounding in his head and the parched feeling in his throat. A sense of impending doom and self-disgust flooded over him. He sat on the edge of the bed trying to remember if he had a court date with a client or not. His mind was fuzzy. He had missed several court appearances in the past few months, which cost him some clients and a scathing note from the district attorney's office. It was starting to damage his reputation.

He staggered from the bedroom out into the hall. He had a sense he was alone in the house. He walked slowly into the kitchen for some vodka and orange juice only to find a note from his wife on the kitchen counter. She had gone with Daniel to her sister's house in New Jersey and didn't know when she'd be coming back—particularly if he was still drinking.

His hands began to tremble. He poured himself a glass of vodka, dumped in a bit of orange juice, and downed it. Then he picked up the phone and called his office. Much to his relief he had no court dates that morning, but he did have a meeting with a new client that afternoon. He downed one more glass of straight vodka, then showered and shaved. He dosed his bloodshot eyes with eye drops and left the house.

It was around noon as he neared his office. His stomach

was growling. He couldn't remember when he had last eaten, so he decided to stop at a local coffee shop. He thought a hot bowl of soup might settle things down.

He slid onto a stool at the lunch counter and ordered a bowl of chicken soup and a cup of coffee. When it arrived, he had trouble getting a spoonful of soup to his mouth. His hands shook so badly that it spilled onto his trousers. That's when he heard, "Bend down and sip it from the bowl. That's what I used to do when I had the shakes."

Joe glanced over and saw a balding man in his seventies sitting next to him with a big smile on his face. He had several missing teeth and a slightly bulbous nose and white stubble growing from his ears. Aside from that he looked in pretty good shape.

"Thanks for the advice," the hungover lawyer replied, "but I don't have the shakes. Just the chills from a little cold."

"That's all right," the old man smiled again. "I used to say the same thing. My name's Hughie by the way, and if Alcoholics Anonymous could get a bum like me sober, it should be a cinch for a young guy like you. Why don't you try it?"

With that, Hughie put a buck tip on the counter and walked slowly from the coffee shop. Joe turned and watched him leave. Suddenly he noticed he was feeling a little better inside. He leaned down and sipped his soup until it was finished. Then he bent over and sipped his coffee.

For some reason, Joe decided to follow the rest of the old man's advice. He went to an AA meeting that night. Much to his surprise he bumped into an old friend at the meeting, a guy named Sammy whom he hadn't seen in several years.

Sammy became his sponsor and led him through the program's Twelve Steps of recovery. Joe never picked up another drink.

For a while, though, he couldn't get Hughie out of his mind. He would look for him at AA meetings. Wherever the lawyer went he would describe the old man and ask if anyone knew him. One night he met a man with many years of sobriety who said he did, but his words were deeply disappointing.

"Yes, Hughie," the old-timer said with a sad smile. "I remember him well. He was a real miracle—a guy right off the streets. He loved AA. He was sober almost a year I think before he started drinking again. I heard they found him dead in a railroad yard about a month ago. Too bad. I was pulling for him."

While the news deeply saddened Joe, he left the meeting that night with a feeling of deep gratitude in his heart for the wonderful, smiling, bald-headed man he met that day at a lunch counter—a man who didn't make it himself but brought God's wonderful miracle of sobriety into Joe's life and into the life of his family.

43
She Was Drowning—Really Drowning

PRACTICALLY EVERY WEEKEND during the summer, Tina's parents would load her and her five siblings into the family station wagon along with a large beach umbrella, beach towels, blankets, plastic inner tubes, pails, shovels, and other paraphernalia. Then they would head off for a place called Jones Beach on Long Island, New York. It was a good hour or so haul from their home in Westchester County, but it was the best white sandy beach around.

She remembers how much fun it was when she was a young girl. She would look forward to the early morning ritual of making tuna fish sandwiches for all the kids, ham and cheese for Dad, and lettuce and tomatoes for Mom. They would wrap them and stuff them into a large red cooler together with iced tea, potato chips, and cookies. Then they were off.

Tina was the middle child. She had two younger sisters and three older brothers. She had just turned nine that particular summer and was trying to show everyone she was all grown up. She was tired of always being teased by her brothers about being afraid of the big waves at the beach and only wanting to sit at the water's edge building sand castles with her little sisters.

The truth was, as much as she enjoyed playing in the surf as it rolled ashore, she wouldn't venture any farther out unless her father or oldest brother, who was a great swimmer, had their arms clamped firmly around her. Only then did she have the courage to duck under a loud, crashing wave with them. Even then she would always hear her mother's voice shouting in their direction, "Watch out for the undertow!"

But now Tina was nine, and it was about time, she thought, to show everyone she was not afraid to face the breaking waves all by herself. So on this particular day, as she waded slowly into the white, foamy water, she was filled with confidence—mainly because she was certain her family was watching her and were all around like a safety net. She didn't realize, however, that the farther she ventured out, the more the undertow was quietly moving her away from her family members. They soon lost sight of her among the crowd of other swimmers.

Tina was soon up to her waist, still feeling confident, however, that she could finally face the pounding surf all by herself. But as she turned to look for her father or one of her brothers, a large wave crashed into her. She lost her balance and plunged beneath the salty foam.

The next few moments seemed like hours. The undertow began carrying her small, thin body farther out from shore. Soon she was in water over her head, trying to touch bottom as more waves crashed over her. Each time she popped to the surface, she saw no help in sight. She was panicking and swallowing so much saltwater that it muffled her screams and cries. She went under, came up, and went under again. Tina was drowning—really drowning.

As her struggling body surfaced one more time, from out of nowhere two enormous hands reached out, grabbed her, and carried her to shore. She tried to see whom the hands belonged to between sobs and coughing up water. She could tell it wasn't a lifeguard and it wasn't her brother or father. All Tina remembered was a tall, strong man with a kind, smiling face looking down at her saying, "You're safe now, sweetheart. I've got you. You're going to be just fine."

He carried her to the water's edge and sat her gently down in the sand. He knelt in front of her holding her hand until she stopped crying. After a few moments, that terrible fear of drowning, of never seeing her family again, began to leave, and a calmness came in its place. She coughed a few more times, spitting up more saltwater, then took a deep breath. She looked around. The man was gone. She stood up and looked around again. He was nowhere in sight. She never had a chance to thank him for saving her life.

Tina ran to the family blanket, where her mother was now doling out the tuna fish sandwiches. No one knew what had just happened to her, so she didn't say a word—perhaps because she didn't want to upset her parents or perhaps because she feared being scolded for not being more careful. And she certainly didn't want to be teased again by her brothers for not being able to swim. She just sat there in silence, eating her tuna fish sandwich and feeling safe and secure in the circle of her family's love and protection.

Even though Tina was only nine at the time, she knew she wasn't saved from drowning simply by accident. She knew from Sunday school all about guardian angels. Deep inside she felt the man who saved her must have been one of God's angels. But she felt disappointed that she never got to thank him, never got his name or where he came from.

As she grew into womanhood, Tina continued to remember her brush with drowning quite vividly. And she became even more grateful to God for saving her life. She would think about all the things she would have missed—dressing up for Halloween, those magical Christmas mornings, coloring Easter eggs, her school graduations and high school prom, the smiles on her parents' faces when she received her college diploma, and her father walking her down the aisle to marry the man of her dreams.

She would not have experienced all that joy, sorrow, and pain—or the love and success that filled her life—had not the strong hands of that stranger come out of nowhere, reached out, pulled her from that boiling surf, and then disappeared again. For that—another of God's quiet, little miracles—Tina remains forever grateful.

44
A Saving Scrap of Paper

AFTER TWO WEEKS on a self-pity drinking binge, Greg had run out of money. He was very sick and had only one place left to go—back home to his mother's house in Chicago, where he knew he would be nourished back to health, something she had done for her only child many times before.

Clara loved her son deeply. It pained her when his wife finally divorced him a few months ago because they were losing everything as a result of his irresponsible drinking. He had lost another good job, they were behind on their mortgage payments, and the loan company was threatening to take their car. So after twelve years of marriage, she threw him out with the clothes on his back, and the divorce court sided with her.

But now even his loving mother was getting tired of wiping his nose and cleaning up after him every time he'd show up at her front door dirty, broke, and hungover. She'd let him sleep it off in his old room, which still looked the same even though Greg was thirty-five years old. There were the old sports posters on the walls, the sports trophies he had won on the dresser, and all the other memorabilia of his growing-up days spread around the bedroom.

The truth was, Clara hated to throw anything away. Her late husband used to say she still had the shoes she wore to her high school prom. That's also why there were always clothes in the closet for Greg to wear, socks and underwear to change into, a nice warm bed to sleep in, and plenty of food to eat. He knew his mother would be there to take care of him whenever he was in trouble.

This time, however, Clara decided to put her foot down. She knew in her heart she wasn't really helping her only child by taking care of him like this. There were no consequences for his bad behavior. Every time he began to feel better, he'd go off and get drunk again. Now she demanded that he do something about his drinking and drugging once and for all or she would not allow him back in her home anymore.

At first Greg was stunned, but before the week was out, he realized that he had to do something to change the course of his life. He knew about Alcoholics Anonymous. His ex-wife once gave him a pamphlet from AA that listed twenty questions that helped define if you were alcoholic or not. Greg threw it away when some of the questions hit too close to home. But now he had to face the truth about himself, particularly since his mother was very serious about her ultimatum. So he called AA's central office, found out where there was a meeting, and went—shakes and all.

That night he heard a recovering alcoholic share his drinking story and the miracle of his recovery. The man, a few years older than Greg, said he had done time in jail for three drunk driving charges. Greg told himself he wasn't that bad since he only had one drunk driving charge. And he had never been in a detox, or had the D.T.'s, or robbed a liquor store as the AA speaker had done. The fact was, Greg really didn't want to be at the meeting, so he barely listened except to compare. When it was over and he was hurrying to get out, an older man grabbed him by the arm and began talking with him.

Greg tried to be polite, but the AA veteran knew he was dealing with a reluctant newcomer. After a few minutes he reached into his pocket, took out a scrap of paper, and wrote down "Pete from AA. Give me a call whenever you need help." Then he stuffed the scrap of paper into Greg's shirt pocket, shook his hand, and walked away.

The next afternoon Clara came home from shopping to find her son drunk again on the living room couch. There was an empty bottle of rye whiskey on the floor. Some of it had spilled onto her new carpeting. She was furious. She shook her son until he finally came to. Then she demanded he pack a suitcase and leave. He didn't even try to argue his case. He staggered into his bedroom, tossed his dirty clothes onto the bed, got dressed, threw some clean clothes into an old suitcase, and left.

Clara stood at her front door in tears, watching her son drive off in his old, beat-up car and wondering whether she was doing the right thing. She hadn't felt such pain since her husband passed away.

Greg had some old drinking buddies in Racine, Wisconsin, about seventy-five miles from Chicago, where he had lived with his ex-wife. They were in the construction business and told him anytime he needed a job, just give them a call. So he headed for Racine.

Five months later, after working on and off and drinking more and more, Greg was sicker than before. Life was miserable. He was hardly eating and was very thin. Even his old drinking buddies had had enough of him and threw him out of their shared condominium. He moved into a roach-infested rooming house. He lived off handouts and the leftovers tossed into Dumpsters by fast-food restaurants.

He woke up one day in his filthy bed knowing he was going to die. He didn't want to die all alone and in such a state. He wanted to die in the arms of the only person he knew still loved him—his mother. But he had sold his jalopy and had no money to travel. How would he get there and would she let him in?

Greg went to his drinking buddies and begged for bus fare back to Chicago. Feeling sorry for their sick friend, they chipped in and gave him the money even though they were sure he'd spend it on another binge. But he didn't. He desperately wanted to get back to his mother's house.

When Clara opened the front door the day her only child arrived, she was appalled by his appearance. She broke down and cried. She helped him wash, put on some clean clothes, have a bit of hot soup, and lay down in his bed. But he was shaking to pieces and feared he was going into the D.T.'s. He pleaded with her to get him some help.

His mother thought she should call for an ambulance. Then she suddenly remembered that scrap of paper she found in her son's shirt pocket the day she was doing his laundry some months back. Since she never threw anything away, she hurried into the kitchen and found that scrap of paper in her writing desk. She called "Pete from AA" and told him her son was very sick from drinking and needed help. Pete was at her home in fifteen minutes.

The AA old-timer sped Greg to an alcohol and drug rehab center only a few miles away where he knew those in charge. They immediately put the trembling alcoholic into the detox ward, where he received medical attention. They saw he was in such bad shape that no one asked about insurance coverage. Clara was able to take care of it later.

Greg stayed at the rehab four months, working diligently on their recovery program, which was based on the Twelve Steps of AA. When he came out, he asked Pete to be his AA sponsor and became an active member in his Chicago group.

That was more than eighteen years ago. Greg has been sober ever since. His life was completely changed by that scrap of paper his Higher Power would not let his mother throw away. He came to know that God certainly does work in some very strange and mysterious ways.

45
Facing Two Fatal Diseases

HE WAS DYING. It might take six months, a year, possibly even two years. But Grant was dying. There was no longer any doubt about it after his family doctor, two pulmonary specialists, a leading oncologist, and twenty-two tests confirmed it. He had advanced pulmonary fibrosis, and it was only a matter of time before his lungs gave out.

A native of Canada, Grant first discovered his condition in September 1993, when his insurance agent was helping him and his partner put together a joint buyout agreement for the steel tire rim manufacturing plant they owned in Calgary. Each required more life insurance as part of the financial package.

The insurance doctor who examined him became concerned about the loud, raspy wheezing he heard coming from Grant's lungs. He said he would need the opinion of a lung specialist before he could approve any expansion of the policy. Grant believed the wheezing was simply the result of smoking too many cigarettes for too many years and agreed to stop. The doctor, on the other hand, suspected it might be the result of breathing in tiny steel shavings from the company's manufacturing process, leaving scar tissue in the bronchial tubes and lower lobes of his lungs. Grant was wrong. The doctor was right.

The concerned businessman spent the next few days drinking rather heavily, which had become a habit of late, especially when it came to facing difficult or troubling situations. At the urging of his partner, he finally went to see his family doctor, who could direct him to a lung specialist. He had a series of chest X-rays taken at a nearby hospital. Both his physician and the pulmonary doctor initially said the X-rays proved inconclusive, that it could possibly be asthmatic bronchitis or advanced emphysema.

Grant's family doctor, however, wanted a second opinion. Since it was late October and the businessman was heading off to his home in Palm Springs, California, where he and his family avoided Calgary's frigid winters, his doctor had a suggestion. He would make an appointment for his patient to see a top pulmonary specialist he knew at Scripps Clinic in San Diego, California, one of the best hospitals in the country for heart-lung diseases. It wasn't that long a drive from Palm Springs, and Grant's physician felt confident they could diagnose and treat whatever the lung problem turned out to be.

It turned out to be advanced pulmonary fibrosis, an idiopathic condition caused by inhaling steel particles for many years. The scar tissue that resulted was depleting his lung capacity and slowly killing him. He was told the only remedy was a lung transplant. The Scripps specialists recommended that he immediately go on oxygen twenty-four hours a day to be more comfortable and to relieve the strain on his weakening lungs. He followed their advice and bought a portable oxygen machine. And he continued drinking to calm his nerves.

Since Grant was a Canadian, the cost for expensive lung transplant surgery would be covered by his native country's socialized medical program. But for that, he would have to have the surgery in Canada. So he called his family doctor to inquire how he should proceed. He was given devastating news. Under his country's highly controversial health insurance plan, he didn't qualify for such surgery. He was too old. The "unwritten" cutoff age was fifty-five, and Grant had just turned sixty.

That weekend he spent drinking himself into oblivion. His wife, a retired nurse, was not only fearful of her husband's lung condition but was now frustrated by his heavy drinking. It was getting out of control. She often wondered aloud which would kill him first—pulmonary fibrosis or his alcoholism, since she well knew they were both fatal diseases.

Despite his alcoholic drinking, Grant never lost his faith in God. In fact, he believed God was his last and only hope. He would drop into the nearby church each day—even though he'd be slightly intoxicated—and beg God to help him. Then he would head off to the Palm Springs Country Club and continue drinking.

A few weeks after Grant received his devastating news, his family doctor called back with a bit of hopeful news. He had spoken with his friend, the pulmonary specialist at Scripps Clinic, and since Grant could afford to pay for the surgery himself, the clinic might consider putting him on their lung transplant list. However, he would first have to pass a battery of tests. Deep inside, Grant had a sense that God was listening to his prayers.

Grant was tense and frightened the day he was to meet with the transplant committee for his initial evaluation. He had a few drinks before leaving home for the drive to San Diego, which greatly upset his wife, who came with him. Everything seemed to go quite well, so when Grant got back to Palm Springs, he went to the country club and had some more drinks to celebrate. When his wife told him not to get his hopes up too high, he got angry and drank even more.

Four days later he received a call from a spokesperson for the transplant committee. He had been turned down as a lung transplant candidate because they found a high level of alcohol in his system. The chief psychiatrist on the committee believed Grant had a serious drinking problem, which would prove detrimental to such delicate surgery.

Once again Grant went into a deep depression. He asked if there were anything he could possibly do to change their opinion. He was told he had the option of returning to Scripps to discuss the matter with the chief psychiatrist. This time he didn't drink before his appointment, but he found it difficult to hide his shaking hands.

The psychiatrist said she might consider changing her recommendation if Grant were willing to enter a local, reputable clinic for treatment of his alcoholism. Once he was sober for a while, she might look at his case again. The businessman knew the psychiatrist's opinion was right just as he knew his wife's opinion had also been right all along. He also sensed that the loving God he had been praying to was trying to do something for him that he couldn't seem to do for himself— stop his drinking.

He spent three months that summer at an alcohol and drug treatment center, where he began his recovery from the fatal disease of alcoholism. He then went faithfully to meetings of Alcoholics Anonymous, where he got a sponsor and worked the program's Twelve Steps of recovery. His wife went back to Calgary in the meantime to be with the rest of their family. She returned to Palm Springs when her husband was notified he had finally been put on the lung transplant waiting list at the Scripps Clinic.

No one knows when donor lungs become available. Grant and his wife had to remain close by the clinic since the call could come suddenly at any time, day or night. So they rented a small condo not far away.

By now the deadly pulmonary fibrosis was well advanced. All they could do was hope and pray for a transplant before time ran out. And hope and pray they did. Whenever Grant was up to it, they would drive to services in the morning at a nearby church and attend an AA meeting at night, always taking the clinic's beeper with them. However, Grant was now on thirteen liters of oxygen per minute and was often too weak to go anywhere.

Then the call came. Grant's wife helped him into the car and drove quickly to the clinic, where they prepped her husband for surgery. Four hours later the transplant team discovered that the prospective donor had a diseased pancreas and the lungs were no good. It was more than a devastating experience for Grant and his wife. It almost made them lose hope.

But they didn't, Grant especially. He clung to his faith in God's love and generosity and prayed even harder as each long day passed. When the beeper finally went off again, he had to be rushed to the hospital by ambulance since he was far too weak to walk. But this time the donor lungs were in excellent condition, although, tragically, they came from a teenage boy killed in a motorcycle accident. (Grant would later learn that doctors at the clinic believed he had possibly only two or three days left to live when he was called into the hospital for surgery.)

The surgery was a complete success. Grant was out of Scripps Clinic in a matter of weeks and playing golf again at his country club in a matter of months. And each time he would stand at the first tee ready to swing his brand-new driver, he would look up and utter another prayer of thanks.

Grant remained forever grateful that his loving Higher Power had healed not only one but two fatal diseases through quiet, little miracles.

46
Saved Twice for a Reason

The fortified castle just outside the town of Valletta in Malta was built by the Knights of Malta back in the Middle Ages to protect the Maltese against an invasion by the Turks. Its gigantic bastions that once overlooked bloody fields today overlook a peaceful valley filled with grazing sheep and goats. It remains a magnet for sightseers.

One warm June evening back in 1959, Camilo, then twelve, was climbing the castle walls with his uncle and aunt, whom he was visiting with that summer. His parents, who had been born in Malta, had sent their son from New York City, where they now lived, to get a taste of their former homeland.

The three climbers had reached the top of one of the bastions and were sitting there staring disappointedly into a cloud-covered sky that made the night as bleak as tar. They had hoped to see the stars, which at this enormous height seemed as if they could be plucked from the sky. But the rains were soon to come, and the heavy clouds were hiding their brilliance.

Camilo's uncle sat on the bastion trying to explain to his

young guest the long history of the castle and the epic stories of its siege. But the young boy soon grew bored and restless. He stood up on the parapet of the bastion and began walking slowly through the darkness. He thought the parapet extended far beyond where they were seated. But it didn't.

He had walked less than ten feet when he suddenly heard his aunt scream out, "Camilo! Stop! Stop!"

The boy froze. He glanced down, and through the darkness managed to see that part of the fortification where he was about to step was missing. It had been blown away by a bomb when the Germans attacked Malta during World War II. Had the young boy taken another step, he would have plunged hundreds of feet to his death.

Strangely enough, Camilo's aunt was completely unaware of the damaged fortification. She hadn't climbed the castle walls in years. To this day she doesn't know why she yelled out that night and saved her nephew's life. On the way back to their village, she told him it must have been God's loving intervention, that God saved the boy for a reason. Camilo believed her.

The memory of that incident and his aunt's comment that God saved him for a reason stayed with Camilo as he grew into adulthood. After graduating from college, he got a job working in social services for the city of New York. Shortly after that he met an attractive young woman named Rose who had just graduated from law school. Ten months later they married.

After scrimping and saving, they managed to buy a small home in a New York suburb, where they hoped to raise a family. Much to their disappointment, Rose discovered a short time later that she couldn't have children. So she focused instead on building a successful law practice. In the meantime, her husband moved from social services into family services and then was appointed director of adoptions for New York City. This led to the couple seriously considering adopting a child.

Since Camilo refused to take advantage of his position, he put his wife and himself on the adoption waiting list. One day he received a call from the head nurse at one of the city's foundling hospitals. She had just taken in a three-month-old boy whose parents had both been killed in a car accident. The nurse, a good friend of the director, teased him, saying that the baby looked just like him and should be taken home to Rose right away.

That's how Tesio became Camilo and Rose's pride and joy. By the time the boy was two, his parents decided they should buy a summer place in the rolling hills of Pennsylvania, where the child could romp and play and might even have a pony. So they bought an old farmhouse and fixed it up. A few days after they moved in, Rose found some ants in the kitchen, some water bugs in the bathroom, and some spiders in her son's bedroom. She called a local exterminator who came late the next afternoon.

The exterminator was a young man who didn't seem to know much about what he was doing. He sprayed the insecticide rather heavily throughout the house. The smell was so strong that Camilo had to open up all the windows. The young man assured them, however, that the bug spray was harmless and that the smell would be gone shortly.

Less than an hour after the exterminator left, it began to pour. The rain was so heavy that Rose and Camilo had to close all the windows. They went to bed early that night since they planned to go out looking for a pony for Tesio the next morning.

It was sometime around 11:00 p.m. when the phone on the night table began ringing. Camilo was in a deep sleep, as was his wife. He reached for the phone and started to cough. He tried sitting up but felt dizzy and sick to his stomach. He finally put the phone to his ear. Someone was calling the wrong number.

As he hung up, he realized there was something terribly wrong with the way he felt. Suddenly it struck him. It must be the insecticide. He could still smell its strong odor in the room. He rushed to the window and opened it. He took several deep breaths of fresh air. Then he woke his wife. She had a difficult time getting to her feet. Then they grabbed their son, wrapped him in a warm blanket, and hurried from the house in their pajamas and bathrobes.

Camilo drove quickly to a nearby hospital, where an emergency room physician checked him and his family. The doctor said they were fortunate to have gotten out of the house before the insecticide had caused any serious harm. He said they would all be fine but to make sure the house was thoroughly aired out before they returned. They then drove to a local motel, where they spent the night. Camilo had difficulty sleeping. He kept thinking about that mistaken phone call so late at night. Was it really someone calling a wrong number— or had it been God calling the right number?

Then came another shock. A few days later, while having breakfast, Rose and her husband read about an older couple in the area dying in their sleep after breathing in the same chemicals that had been sprayed in their home. It wasn't long after that they heard that the exterminating company involved went out of business. The news convinced Camilo that God had saved his life once again. But why? He remembered the incident in Malta. Why did God perform these two quiet miracles that so greatly impacted his life? He knew there must be a reason.

Today Camilo believes he knows the reason. He's convinced his loving God wanted him to adopt a little baby boy who had tragically lost his parents, to raise and educate him so that he could graduate from medical school and become a fine doctor—not just a doctor—but a life-saving heart surgeon.

Camilo and Rose's adopted son, Tesio, is one of the country's foremost heart surgeons, creating innovative surgical techniques that continue to save hundreds and hundreds of lives each year. And he enjoys listening to his father tell the stories of God's miracles over and over again.

47
No More Bull

Even taking pain pills with a double shot of Jack Daniels wasn't working anymore. And those busted ribs and torn tendons weren't healing as fast as they used to. Add that to his arthritic knees and hips, and you didn't have to be an orthopedic surgeon to know that Bubby's days of riding bulls on the rodeo circuit were over. At the age of thirty-seven, he was just another washed-up, over-the-hill cowboy.

It had been a long and exciting ride. His mortgaged-to-the-hilt ranch house in Taos, New Mexico, was filled with blue ribbons, first-place trophies, and commendations from three state governors. Still, most of the money that those ribbons, trophies, and honors represented was gone. Three failed marriages, a pile of medical bills, and his heavy drinking and drugging helped pave the trail to near-bankruptcy. It was only a matter of time before his creditors came calling.

He would sit in sleazy saloons bragging to other drunks about his glory days. For a while his reputation as a pretty good bull rider garnered him a lot of free drinks. Then his growing reputation as a freeloader and ornery drunk started getting him thrown out of more saloons than allowed him in.

Finally Bubby lost his ranch house in Taos to the tax collector. He began moving from one dead-end job to another. First he drove and branded cattle and mended fences. Then he cooked for ranch hands and cleaned up the bunkhouse. In between he spent some time in the hospital for back surgery so that he could walk and time in jail for being drunk and disorderly.

By the time the former bull rider turned forty, he was a lost and bewildered man willing to do whatever it took to get another pint of booze. That's when he first met Galen, the pastor of a small church in Carson City, Nevada. Bubby had been following the rodeo and was selling programs at the arena there to make a few bucks.

One night he staggered into a small Laundromat in town to wash some of his dirty clothes. As he sat there waiting for them to dry, he spotted a nice-looking, clean-cut man seated nearby reading what appeared to be a spiritual book.

That God stuff, Bubby thought to himself. *That never got me anywhere even when I used to pray. At this point, I'm sure God don't want anything to do with a low-down bum like me.*

The thought had only crossed his mind when the clean-cut stranger walked over and sat across from him. He smiled and asked Bubby how he was doing, as if he couldn't tell by his appearance.

"I've seen better days," the washed-up cowboy replied. "Why do you ask?"

"I happen to be a minister," the man smiled, "a minister

whose congregation is so small he has to do his own laundry as you can see. But, well, last night I had a dream that someone in serious trouble might need my help. Tell me, is there anything I can do for you?"

"Sure," Bubby smiled back. "I'm down on my luck, so if you got a few bucks to spare, I could use it."

"My hunch is you'd only blow it on alcohol," the minister responded. "Am I right?"

The former bull rider didn't reply. He simply grinned and nodded. Then when the minister asked if they might pray together so that God could touch his heart and show him a better life, Bubby got up and walked away. Galen understood. He went and opened a dryer, stuffed his laundry into a duffel bag, and headed for the door. He hesitated, then turned and walked back to Bubby.

"If I offended you in any way, I'm sorry," he said very kindly. "If you're ever in the market for real help, my church is 'The Spirit of God' just three blocks down the road." Then he left.

Six months later the former bull rider found himself coming off another binge in Medford, Oregon. Somehow he had gotten a job there at a lumber mill but soon drank his way out of it. Stopping at a local saloon, he heard they were looking for lumberjacks near Grants Pass about thirty miles away. He thumbed his way to the edge of town but couldn't go on any farther.

At this point in his life he was beaten down more than ever before. He sat at the side of the road shaking and sweating. He felt hopeless and afraid. He had heard about "hitting bottom," and he felt he was there. Perhaps it was that moment of sheer desperation that made him look up into the clear blue sky and murmur, "God, I know you're up there. Please come down and give me a hand. I can't go on like this anymore."

He sat there for another few minutes until he caught his breath. Then he pushed himself erect and continued down the road. He hadn't gone more than a half mile when he noticed a small, white church just up ahead. *Maybe they'll give me something to eat,* he thought to himself. *Maybe they'll even let me rest there for a while.*

Bubby went around to the back door of the church and knocked. After a moment a rather pleasant elderly lady appeared. She told him if he needed any help he would have to see the minister, who lived in the cottage just across the street. He thanked her and started walking slowly toward the pretty cottage with a green roof and red chimney.

As he approached, he spotted a man in the backyard tending to some flowers and shrubbery. He stopped at the white fence. He coughed softly a few times to get the man's attention. When the man turned around, Bubby's mouth fell open and his eyes filled with tears. It was Galen, the minister he met that night at the Laundromat in Carson City. Despite his befogged brain, he knew that God had answered his simple prayer and somehow knew that everything was going to be all right.

Galen, who was also stunned, had a similar feeling—that God was giving him still another opportunity to help someone very much in need. He brought the sick and shaking cowboy into his home, where his wife gave the hungry man something to eat and drink. They talked about the wonderful way God works, that after Galen's small church in Nevada was forced to close due to the lack of financial support, he was invited to be the pastor of this church in Grants Pass. And now a man he tried to offer God's help to months ago miraculously showed up on his doorstep.

Before inviting Bubby to spend some time with them until he got back on his feet, the minister had one more of God's quiet, little miracles to offer him. He said the fellowship of Alcoholics Anonymous held meetings at his church three nights a week. There would be one the following evening, and he urged Bubby to attend.

Not only did Bubby attend the AA meeting, but he also joined the AA group and got a sponsor. God's love and AA's Twelve Steps of recovery got Bubby sober and kept him sober. They enabled him to find a new way of life and the kind of happiness he never knew existed. He would often say at meetings that there was no more bull in his life and he was finally glad of it.

48
A Taxing Situation

MOST PEOPLE HAVE a tendency to think about God only as an expert when it comes to spiritual matters. Terry discovered, much to his good fortune, that God is an expert at everything—even a really messed up financial situation such as the one he found himself in after ten years of alcoholic drinking.

He had been sober now in Alcoholics Anonymous for almost eight months but still couldn't find a job in Pittsburgh that paid enough to support his wife and their three young children. He had worked in the banking industry until he was fired six years before for absenteeism and misconduct, both a result of his heavy drinking. Since then he had five different jobs, none of them lasting more than a year. At the age of thirty-two, he found himself unemployable until finally joining the fellowship of AA and sobering up. He then started work at a collection agency, pestering people for money they didn't have. He hated it but needed a paycheck.

With all the kids now in school, Terry's wife had recently

taken a part-time secretarial position with a small firm. But together, the amount of money both were bringing home after taxes was barely enough to pay for the rent, their other bills, and food for the table. The former banker was almost at his wit's end when a man he had befriended at his AA group approached him one night after a meeting. He knew Terry's predicament and asked if he were willing to move to another state to get a better job.

It seems the man had a very good friend who was the head of the actuarial department at a large insurance company headquartered in Knoxville, Tennessee. His friend was looking for a young assistant actuary. Terry's AA buddy thought his banking experience might qualify him for the well-paying position. Since he was only sober eight months, the young man sought his AA sponsor's advice.

He was told that as long as there were good AA meetings in Knoxville—and there were—that this could well be God offering him an opportunity to get back on his feet. His sponsor said he should turn the matter over to his Higher Power and pray on it.

Terry was indeed ready to move, but because he was only sober eight months, his wife was reluctant at first to be so far away from her family and friends. After all the heartbreak, fear, and disappointment she had been through, she was only beginning to trust her husband's word, his coming home at night for dinner, and his improving relationship with their children.

The good thing was that Terry's wife was attending Al-Anon meetings, a recovery program for families. She was also advised by several women at her meeting that she put the situation in God's hands and be willing to accept the outcome.

So she flew down to Knoxville with her husband and toured the city while he went for his job interview. The interview went extremely well. The head of the actuarial department liked the young former banker and introduced him to many on his staff. Also, because he respected and trusted the man Terry knew in his AA group, the executive did only a cursory background check before offering him the position.

Terry and his family moved to Knoxville right after Christmas. His wife and children were excited, but there was one big problem that still loomed over his head, one big skeleton in his closet that he had never shared with his sponsor, either out of fear or lack of trust. Now, as he and his family looked forward to a new life and brighter future, the skeleton really began to haunt him.

It seems he hadn't filed his income tax returns for the past eight years, ever since his alcoholism took control of his life and made it unmanageable. Every time he would receive a letter from the Internal Revenue Service, he would toss it into the garbage. He would wake up some nights with cold sweats, fearing the feds would soon be coming to drag him off to prison. Those nightmares were now coming more often.

As he became active in AA in Knoxville and got another sponsor there, Terry knew he had to share his fears before they drove him back to drinking. So he asked his new sponsor to join him for a cup of coffee one night after a meeting. They went to a local diner, where he broke down and told the man the whole story. His sponsor, a man in his late fifties, said he had heard a whole lot worse over his twenty-five years of sobriety in AA. He also told his young sponsee that he understood his fears but that he had to put his trust in his Higher Power. He said God would find a way to work things out.

The very next day Terry's new sponsor called him at work. There was someone he wanted him to meet—another AA member who might be able to help with this "taxing" situation. That was an understatement and the beginning of two quiet, little miracles God was about to perform in Terry's life. You see, the AA member his sponsor was talking about just happened to be the deputy director of the Internal Revenue Service in Knoxville.

At lunch a few days later, Terry sat open-mouthed and wide-eyed while the deputy director, a very kind and warm man in his early sixties, told him he fully understood how these things can happen, especially with alcoholics and their messed-up financial lives. Then he explained what he wanted his luncheon companion to do. He had to gather whatever past financial information he had on his income and deductions and send them to his office at the federal building. In the interim, the IRS official said he would further investigate the matter himself.

Terry could find very little financial data from the past. So he sat down and wrote the deputy director a letter reconstructing as best he could the jobs he once held and the approximate income he received. He knew the letter wouldn't be much help, but it was the best he could do.

Several weeks went by, and he heard nothing. It seemed like several years. He was reluctant to bug his sponsor, knowing he would be told to "turn it over" and "trust God." Terry was also reluctant to tell his wife what was happening for fear it might reignite her lack of trust in him. She had long since stopped asking about back taxes because there had been so many more pressing problems in their lives. He decided to wait for the outcome, no matter how it turned out.

Then the day came when God was ready to perform His second quiet miracle in Terry's life. The deputy director called and asked him to come by his office the next afternoon. He feared the worst. His mind was buzzing with all sorts of scenarios as he walked into the large government office building and made his way to the elevators. Perhaps he could borrow whatever he would need from his parents or ask his wealthy uncle to cosign a bank note or maybe beg the IRS to let him pay them over a period of years.

When he walked into the deputy director's office that day, never in his wildest dreams could he have expected to hear the words he heard.

"I did the best I could for you, Terry," the IRS executive said with a serious look on his face. Terry braced himself for the terrible news he was sure was about to come.

"The big problem was your lack of financial information, particularly when it came to any tax deductions," the director continued. "However, I did manage to put together your total income over that period of time and the amount the government took out of your various paychecks."

Then the tax official smiled and said, "After all the fixed penalties for not filing your tax returns on time, it seems like the IRS owes you $1,695."

Terry couldn't have appeared any more shocked than if he had been struck by lightning. The deputy director, who was also his AA compatriot, came around his desk, reached out, and placed the check in the young man's trembling hands. Then, as he shook his hand, he said very softly, "God sure does work in strange ways, doesn't He?"

That night Terry put the check into his wife's hands. His eyes were moist as he told her again how sorry he was for all the lies, all the covering up, all the hurt and mistrust he had brought into her life. He asked her to forgive him. She did because she knew that's what God wanted her to do. They had both now turned their wills and their lives over to a Power greater than themselves. And they were grateful to that Power for the quiet miracles that changed their lives.

49
A Father's Serenity
Resurrected Her Faith

IT WOULD BE hard to find more tragedy in a single family than Alice had in hers. Perhaps it's understandable, then, why this once quite religious lady with three troubled sons gradually lost her faith in God and why she found it so difficult to get it back again.

Her trail of woe began on December 14, 1973, when her oldest son, Randy, who was seventeen at the time, learned that his sixteen-year-old girlfriend, Laura, whom he adored, had been brutally murdered. To make matters worse, the police arrested him for killing her. The girl had been beaten, raped, stabbed twenty-six times, and then thrown off a cliff in the Azusa Canyon in southern California. After eleven hours of harsh grilling by detectives, the teenager was released after the dead girl's ex-boyfriend confessed to murdering her in a jealous rage.

When Alice and her husband were finally able to drive their son home, he collapsed in the driveway as he was getting out of the car. They couldn't revive him, so they called for medical help. The paramedics couldn't get a pulse, so they rushed the teenager to the hospital, where he lay in a coma for three weeks. The doctors called it emotional trauma, when someone can't handle the pain and reality of a tragic situation.

After coming out of his coma, Randy was kept in the psychiatric ward of the hospital for several weeks to undergo treatment. He seemed much better when he came home. In fact, Alice recalls her son sitting next to her on the living room sofa and saying, "You always told us boys that out of every bad thing that happens to us, some good will come from it. I couldn't imagine what good could come from Laura's murder, but now I think I know."

"Tell me," his mother replied.

"Everybody has some kind of tragedy in their lives. I'm only seventeen, and I've already had mine, so I don't have to worry about something like that ever happening again."

Two days later his father, whom he was very close to, died of a massive heart attack. The whole family was devastated, especially Alice's oldest son. This time Randy handled the tragedy a different way. He started drinking and drugging, including mainlining heroin and smoking crack. For Alice, things got even worse when her other two sons, ages fourteen and sixteen, followed in their older brother's footsteps.

As her painful burdens increased, Alice tried to cling to her faith. She begged God to help her sons and to give her the strength and the direction to deal with their addictions as best she could. But things only got worse. Over the next two years, her sons and their alcohol- and drug-addicted friends stole practically everything of any value from her home to support their habits.

She would change the locks on her doors, but they would break in, sometimes in the middle of the night, and almost frighten her to death. That's when she started getting orders of protection against her own sons, sometimes being forced to put them in jail for several days, hoping they would change. Alice didn't believe things could get any worse. But they did.

Not only was this heartbroken mother now getting angry at God for allowing all this tragedy in her life, but she began drinking herself to relieve her emotional pain and find oblivion. Before long she was at the bars practically every night. The good job she had gotten after her husband died was now in jeopardy. All the money from their savings and insurance policies was starting to dwindle. She continued to worry frantically about her sons as their addictions got even worse. She knew she was powerless to help them, and even her friends said she could only help herself—and she should do it before she lost everything.

Alice considered making a geographic change. She thought moving from Los Angeles to Rancho Mirage, which was out in the California desert, might ease her mind and change the way she was living. She and her husband used to vacation there at a resort, and she still had some friends in the area. So she sold her large home in L.A. and bought a three-bedroom condo in Rancho Mirage, hoping some of her boys might come with her. They refused, so she bought them a small condo in Studio City. She thought it would ease her guilt for leaving them behind.

Still angry at God, the frustrated woman now took charge of her own life. She felt sure the move would make everything better. At forty-four, she was still a young and rather attractive woman. She would find a nice job, meet a nice man, get married again, and have a nice life. But she still continued to drink, rather heavily at times, and the more she did, the more her daydreams began to fade.

Soon it became vodka and orange juice in the morning, scotch and sodas at the bars in the afternoon, and a bottle of wine or two at home with dinner—that is, if she was able to make it that far. Many nights she passed out before dinner. She had long since stopped praying, asking for help or guidance. It was her will now. She was running the show. That's when her faith in a loving God simply faded away—or so it seemed.

When Alice heard that her oldest son had been arrested for his third drunk driving charge and was going to jail for six months, she drank more. When her middle son was arrested on burglary charges and was on probation for a year, she drank more. When her youngest son stopped talking to her because she wouldn't give him any more money, she drank more.

Two of her best friends in the desert had been urging her for months to get help for her drinking. It was only after the distraught mother had to be rushed to the emergency room one night after falling outside a bar and cutting her head open did she finally surrender. She accepted the fact that she had a serious drinking problem. After leaving the hospital, she called Alcoholics Anonymous and went to her first AA meeting in Palm Springs.

It wasn't easy, however. Alice was embarrassed to be there. After preaching for years to her addicted sons, she felt she had now fallen to their level. She had difficulty accepting alcoholism as a disease, that she was actually powerless over what she drank to ease her pain. And she was still angry at a God she said she no longer believed in. Now she had to hear everyone in AA talking about a "Higher Power." She knew that for many this meant God, and it only confused and frustrated her more.

Alice continued to struggle with the AA program and its Twelve Steps of recovery. She didn't get a sponsor. She would sit in the back of the meeting room and fidget every time someone talked about spirituality. One week she would admit she was powerless over alcohol and the next week deny it. Soon she was drinking again, trying to control it without much success.

Then, weaving her way home from a bar one afternoon, she was arrested for drunk driving and taken to jail. A woman in AA who had befriended her, always telling her the program would work in her life if she gave it time, came to the jail and bailed her out. Alice was mortified, but now finally convinced that she was an alcoholic. She asked the woman to be her AA sponsor.

But it still wasn't easy. Alice just couldn't forget all the tragedy in her life and her anger against God for not being there when she needed Him most. Why did He let her son's girlfriend die in such a brutal manner? Why did He take her husband, a man she loved and leaned on for support? Why did He allow all her sons to become such terrible addicts? How could she ever have faith again in that kind of a Higher Power?

God was about to give her the answer.

One day, still struggling to stay sober, Alice received a wedding invitation in the mail from an old friend in Los Angeles. They had been close for years. The friend's daughter was to be married, and she very much wanted Alice to be there. Since the wedding was on a Sunday, her sponsor strongly suggested she attend an AA meeting the night before.

There happened to be an AA clubhouse not far from the hotel in Los Angeles where Alice decided to spend that weekend. On Saturday night there was an open speaker meeting. When she arrived, the place was quite crowded. Someone mentioned that a lady with many years of sobriety was to be the speaker that night. Alice looked forward to hearing her. However, as the hour drew near for the meeting to begin, the lady hadn't arrived. So the secretary for the group asked a man she knew to speak in her place. He nervously agreed.

As the man began to tell his painful tale of alcoholic drinking and his miraculous recovery in AA, Alice was taken by the peace in his eyes and his ability to laugh at the many hard bumps on his road to alcohol dependence and a life of unmanageability. She laughed right along with him at his sometimes almost preposterous "drunk-a-log"—that is, until be began telling the tragic story of the brutal murder of his sixteen-year-old daughter, Laura. The room went absolutely silent.

Alice leaned forward in her chair. As she listened to the heartfelt words coming from this sober man's lips, she suddenly realized he was the father of her oldest son's girlfriend—the father she only met once at the funeral. She hardly recognized him. That agonizing look on his face back then was completely gone. There was a serene look in its place. She started to understand as he went on to say that he only found that peace and serenity by turning his will and his life over to the loving God he found in the program of AA. Alice fell to pieces. She began to sob.

Watching and listening through her tears to this father speak so calmly about the biggest tragedy in his life, Alice was deeply touched. She knew at that moment that God had led her here this night to help her understand that she, too, could find peace in the midst of heartbreak, that while her Higher Power allowed bad things to happen, He was also a God of love who could make good things come from them. All she had to do was what this once unhappy and helpless alcoholic father did: turn her will and her life over to the care of this loving God.

After the meeting, Alice waited until most of the people had thanked the speaker and left. Then she approached him and said, trying to hold back more tears, "Hi. My name is Alice. I'm Randy's mother."

For a brief moment a look of surprise combined with a touch of pain appeared in the speaker's eyes. Then he smiled, reached out, and hugged Alice, saying, "Isn't it wonderful? We don't have to be sad anymore."

They went for a cup of coffee and talked for several hours. Laura's father promised he would try to contact Randy and her other two sons. He kept his promise.

A few months later, when Randy got out of jail, he came into AA and got clean and sober. Before the year was out, his two younger brothers once again followed in his footsteps. Today Alice and her sons are sober and active in the fellowship of AA. And they all have a very strong faith in a loving Higher Power.

50
Looking Back with Gratitude

AMERICA WILL NEVER forget the horror of September 11, 2001, when nineteen terrorists took control of four commercial airliners, crashing two into New York's Twin Towers, bringing down both stately skyscrapers, crashing another into the Pentagon, and the fourth into a field in Pennsylvania after passengers foiled an attempt to crash into the White House or U.S. Capitol. The attacks killed 2,974 innocent people.

That terrible tragedy ignited frightful memories for many all over the world and especially for one particular couple who used to live in Munich, Germany—Germany being a country that has suffered more than its share of terrorist attacks.

Today that couple, Peggy and Trinidad, reside in the United States. They look back with gratitude whenever they recall their own brush with unspeakable violence, for they know it was their Higher Power that saved them from death that fateful day.

It was the evening of September 26, 1980, just one year before they emigrated to America. The world famous beer festival in Munich had just begun. People were pouring into the city from all across Europe to sing and dance and eat and drink huge steins of German beer. Peggy and Trinidad were looking forward to celebrating with their many friends as they did each year.

There was only one difference this particular year—a slight conflict with their social calendar. Where normally they would stay at the exciting festival until very late in the evening, this year they had to make a long trip the next day and needed an early start. A close relative was getting married and their daughter was to be the flower girl and their son the ring bearer. Since it was a morning wedding almost one hundred miles away, they would have to leave by dawn.

So the couple planned to arrive at what is commonly called "Oktoberfest" around 6:00 p.m. and leave no later than 10:00 p.m. This way they could enjoy themselves and still get a few hours of sleep. Also, when they arrived, Trinidad decided to park their car several blocks away from the "official" area to avoid any possibility of getting caught up in a traffic jam later at the exits from the huge parking fields.

Most of the couple's many friends from work and their neighborhood were already there partying in one of the many gigantic tents set up to accommodate thousands of revelers. A big brass band was playing loudly. People were singing even more loudly. The tables were overflowing with food, and pretty waitresses in colorful skirts were carrying large, foaming steins of German beer to thirsty customers.

Peggy and Trinidad joined right in with the festivities, forgetting all about the time. They sang and danced and ate and agreed with all their friends that this was the best Oktoberfest Munich ever held, and it attracted the largest crowd in the history of the annual event.

It was after 9:45 p.m. when Peggy first nudged her husband. She pointed to her wristwatch and whispered that perhaps they should start saying their good-byes to their fellow merrymakers. Also, it was a long walk to where they parked the car and a twenty-minute drive home.

Her husband agreed. But as he stood and began waving good night to everyone, a man who worked for him at the industrial firm he managed wanted to discuss a business matter. Then another from his company wanted to discuss the upcoming labor contract. Trinidad glanced at his own watch. It was close to 10:00 p.m. He tried to pull himself away when two other men approached and started a conversation.

He glanced over at his wife and saw she was getting rather exasperated. Finally, she walked over, grabbed her husband by the arm, and started pulling him gently toward the front entrance of the tent, where they had entered earlier. She apologized to those nearby, saying they had an early trip to make the next morning and were sorry they had to leave. She was making progress just as a waitress approached with more steins of beer. Trinidad had to have one more for the road. He guzzled it down and finally headed toward the exit with his wife.

They were only a few feet from the exit when they suddenly heard a massive, deafening explosion outside the tent, not five hundred feet from where they were standing. The noise and shock pushed them back into a table. They saw smoke and flames billowing skyward and people yelling and screaming as they ran in all directions. Panic filled the tent. Everyone headed en masse toward the rear exit. Peggy and Trinidad followed them.

The couple was shaking and sweating as they hurried toward the street where they had parked their car. They began to hear the blaring sirens of police cars, emergency vehicles, and ambulances. Then in the distance came the loud horns and clanging bells of fire engines as the terrible, bloodcurdling screams from the injured started to fade away. Glancing back toward the flames, Peggy and Trinidad knew there was nothing they could possibly do to help in the midst of what was obviously a terribly destructive incident.

They jumped into their car and began circling through the unfamiliar neighborhood trying to avoid the massive traffic rushing from the festival grounds. Once they got on a familiar boulevard and headed home, Trinidad turned on the radio and found a station that gave weather, traffic information, and local news. The newscaster had little information except that an apparent bomb had been triggered outside one of the festival's largest tents. He had no death toll but said hundreds of injured were being taken to twenty-three hospitals in the Munich area.

It was close to midnight when Peggy and Trinidad finally got home. Their middle-aged babysitter hugged them. She had heard about the horrible incident and feared they might have been hurt. When she left, they turned on their television set. Germany's chancellor Helmut Schmidt was speaking at a press conference. He explained that a terrorist had detonated a large explosive device in a trash barrel at Oktoberfest. More than a dozen people were known dead, and hundreds were critically injured, many losing arms and legs from shrapnel. The chancellor said a well-known terrorist organization had already taken credit for the heinous act, demanding the German government change its conservative policies.

It wasn't until the following morning on their way to the wedding that they learned more of the tragic details and saw the gruesome photos of the dead and injured in a local newspaper. But by then, Peggy and Trinidad had recognized how fortunate they were.

Just before going to bed after listening to the chancellor on TV, Peggy was setting the alarm clock. She stopped, held the clock in her hand, and glanced over at her husband. He knew exactly what she was thinking. If their timing had been a little different, they would have been walking right through the area where the terrorist's bomb exploded. They would have surely been killed or maimed. Peggy's eyes filled with tears. Then she knelt down beside her bed and started to pray. Trinidad joined her.

As each year passes and more random terrorist incidents occur, this particular couple from Munich, Germany, continue to look back with gratitude, for they both know that they were saved that fateful day through a quiet miracle.

Postscript

AFTER YOU CONTEMPLATE the inspiring stories contained in this book, it is my hope that your knowledge, relationship, and faith in a Higher Power will be strengthened and increased.

Some may still consider these events to be coincidences. Still, the impact and power they had on those involved and the way they changed hearts and lives must make one pause and wonder.

It is my belief that God's grace touches everyone. Perhaps one or more of these miracle stories made you recall a similar or comparable incident in your own life. If you would like to share it—one or more—large or small—openly or anonymously—please write it down and send it to

William G. Borchert
P.O. Box 538
Little River, SC 29566

Or e-mail it to

williamgborchert@aol.com

Thank you.

About the Author

WILLIAM G. BORCHERT was nominated for an Emmy for writing the highly acclaimed Warner Brothers/Hallmark Hall of Fame movie *My Name Is Bill W.*, which starred James Garner, James Woods, and JoBeth Williams. In addition to being a screenwriter, he is also a film producer and well-known author.

Bill began his writing career as a journalist, working first as a reporter for one of New York City's largest daily newspapers. Later, as a byline feature writer, he covered many of the nation's most important news stories from racial strife in the South to the start of the Space Age to the country's last execution in an electric chair.

After writing for a major media wire service and a national magazine and creating syndicated shows for radio, Bill became a partner at Artists Entertainment Complex, a new independent film and talent management company that went on to produce a number of box office hits. These included *Kansas City Bomber* starring Raquel Welch, *Serpico* starring Al Pacino, and *Dog Day Afternoon* also starring Al Pacino.

A member of the Writers Guild of America and a director of the Stepping Stones Foundation, he has written and co-written a number of books, including *The Lois Wilson Story* and *Sought Through Prayer and Meditation.* He also has several other movie projects in development including another Hallmark Hall of Fame movie based on his book *The Lois Wilson Story.*

Bill and his wife, Bernadette, travel extensively, speaking to groups large and small all across the country about recovery from alcoholism, a fatal disease that continues to affect millions of men and women and their families. When they are not traveling or spending time with their nine children and twenty-three grandchildren, you will find Bill writing at the computer in his office and Bernadette painting at the easel in her studio.

A former resident of New York, the author and his wife now live in a lovely home on a golf course in Little River, South Carolina, only fifty yards from the eighteenth fairway and only a few minutes drive to the Carolina coast.

Hazelden, a national nonprofit organization founded in 1949, helps people reclaim their lives from the disease of addiction. Built on decades of knowledge and experience, Hazelden offers a comprehensive approach to addiction that addresses the full range of patient, family, and professional needs, including treatment and continuing care for youth and adults, research, higher learning, public education and advocacy, and publishing.

A life of recovery is lived "one day at a time." Hazelden publications, both educational and inspirational, support and strengthen lifelong recovery. In 1954, Hazelden published *Twenty-Four Hours a Day,* the first daily meditation book for recovering alcoholics, and Hazelden continues to publish works to inspire and guide individuals in treatment and recovery, and their loved ones. Professionals who work to prevent and treat addiction also turn to Hazelden for evidence-based curricula, informational materials, and videos for use in schools, treatment programs, and correctional programs.

Through published works, Hazelden extends the reach of hope, encouragement, help, and support to individuals, families, and communities affected by addiction and related issues.

For questions about Hazelden publications, please call **800-328-9000** or visit us online at **hazelden.org/bookstore**.